EAT!

100+ Easy Vegetarian Recipes You'll Make Again and Again

By Sarah Bond
BSc Nutrition, MSc Food Science
creator of live eat learn

Eat! 100+ Easy Vegetarian Recipes You'll Make Again and Again.

Self-published

This book may be purchased in bulk at special discounts for sales promotion, corporate gifts, fund-raising, or educational purposes. Special editions can also be created to specifications. For details, contact sarah@liveeatlearn.com.

Book design by Sarah Bond

Author photographs by Molly Bond

Photographs on pages 8, 9, and 133 by Mitch and Justine Chapman

All other photography by Sarah Bond

With editing help from George and Lori Bond

Hardcover Print ISBN: 979-8-9904833-2-3

Ebook ISBN: 979-8-9904833-9-2

Printed in China

For our Readers & our Eaters

CONTENTS

Introduction

I haven't always been someone who cooks. But I've always been someone who eats.

So, if you, like me, love to eat, this book is made for you.

Some people see cooking as the main event. For me, cooking was always the means to the end: eating, and eating well.

I thought I had a grasp on the concept of "cooking" after graduating with my bachelor's degree in nutrition, flung into the adult world and suddenly having to cook for myself. I understood the fundamentals of what makes food healthy, so I should be able to make healthy food. Right?

But I had no idea how to turn the ingredients I brought home from the supermarket into a dish worth eating.

And so, as a creative outlet and to document my learning to cook, I started my vegetarian food blog, Live Eat Learn.

The concept was simple: pick a random ingredient at the grocery store and spend a week learning how to cook with it, from classic dishes to recipes that break all the rules.

Ten years later, Live Eat Learn has become one of the most popular vegetarian food sites on the web. I've developed over 1,000 easy vegetarian recipes feeding millions of readers every month, from lifelong vegetarians to folks just dabbling in eating less meat.

Oh, and the best part? I know how to cook now. In my pursuit of creating food that makes me—and, most importantly, our readers—want to clean their plates, I eventually went back to school for my master's degree in sensory science.

This type of food science focuses on how people perceive food through taste, smell, texture, and appearance. It's all about using people's preconceived perceptions of food to create something delicious. While many of my friends from school now work in the food industry, helping to develop the food products you see in your grocery stores, I use my background in sensory science to develop recipes for you!

Put simply: I love food, I love to eat, and in case you feel the same, here are over 100 of our most reader-loved, rigorously-tested vegetarian recipes.

About The Recipes

When I develop a recipe, there are three things I want to achieve:

Make it easier

There's something you should know about me. I am not a patient person. And for better or for worse (okay, I'm biased, but it's definitely for better), my lack of patience is reflected in my recipes. Because in my quest to get good food on plates, there isn't time to get lost in wordy instructions or complicated steps.

Make it healthier

The word "healthy" means many different things to many different people, but my background in nutrition laid the foundation for how I create recipes: plant-forward, healthy fats, whole grains, lots of herbs and seasonings, and plant-based proteins. I've included basic nutrition information for each recipe, but please note that these are estimates and should be treated as such.

Make it vegetarian

My goal with Live Eat Learn is to create recipes that help you eat more veggies and stop missing meat on your plate. Whether that means creating an epic grain bowl that celebrates plants or recreating the perfect vegetarian meatloaf, I try to create recipes for folks at every stage in their plant-based journey.

What's in this book?

Eat! That's what I want for you.

Not **"Only Cook On Weekends Because I Don't Have Time!"**

Not **"Flip Through Recipes And Get Overwhelmed!"**

Not **"Cooking 3 Separate Meals Because My Family Won't Eat That!"**

I want you and your people to eat, and eat well, so this book includes over 100 tried-and-tested easy vegetarian recipes.

Have a question about a recipe? Scan the QR codes throughout the book with your phone, which will take you to the recipe on my site. You can drop a question at the end of the post (I personally respond to these daily).

Most of the recipes in this book are dinners because this always seems to be the meal for which I need extra inspiration. The breakfasts in this book are choose-your-adventure-style (because who doesn't love to start their day with an adventure?). For lunch, I've included some of my favorite entree and side dish pairings, which are perfect for meal prepping.

So, let's eat!

Favorite Ingredients

There are a few ingredients you'll find often in this book. They're staples in my kitchen!

Chickpeas (Garbanzo Beans)

You may think this book is about vegetarian recipes—and it is—but really, it's about chickpeas. Chickpeas stand out for their versatility and health benefits. Rich in protein, fiber, vitamins, and minerals like iron, folate, and manganese, they support digestive health and help maintain a balanced diet. And as you'll soon find out, I put them in everything.

To peel or not to peel? While you can certainly pluck off the loose skins of the chickpeas before using them in your recipe, peeling takes too much time in my opinion. I typically leave the skins on!

All the recipes in this book call for canned chickpeas, but cooking them yourself from dried is easy and economical. 1 (15-ounce) can of chickpeas equals 1 ½ cups cooked chickpeas.

Sort to remove any bad chickpeas and debris, then rinse.

Add chickpeas to a pot of salted water.

Cover and simmer for 1 ½ to 2 hours

Mushrooms

Mushrooms are one of my favorite ingredients because of their umami taste, which adds depth and richness to vegetarian dishes. They also contain protein, fiber, antioxidants, and B vitamins. Whether sautéed, grilled, or used as a meat substitute, mushrooms offer a meaty texture and savory flavor we love. Plus, there are so many types to explore!

Quinoa

Quinoa is a complete protein source, containing all nine essential amino acids, which is rare in the plant world. It's also high in fiber, B vitamins, and minerals. Quinoa's subtle nutty flavor and ability to absorb flavors make it a great base for salads and bowls!

Rinse quinoa to remove natural bitter coating.

Add 2 cups water and 1 cup quinoa to a pot.

Simmer for 10 to 15 minutes, until tender.

Tofu

Tofu is a fantastic plant-based protein source, rich in calcium and iron, and can take on countless flavors and textures, making it incredibly versatile. From silken to extra firm, tofu can be scrambled, baked, or blended into smoothies, offering a substantial protein boost.

Tofu typically comes in either a 14- or 16-ounce block. The recipes in this book all note to use a 14-ounce block, but 16 ounces should also work!

Pressing improves texture and flavor, allowing the tofu to absorb more flavor in cooking.

Drain tofu and wrap in paper towels or clean kitchen towles.

Place a heavy object on the tofu for 15 to 30 minutes.

Use as directed in the recipe.

Olive Oil

Olive oil is my go-to all-purpose oil, and I love it for its flavor and health benefits. As long as you're not cooking with high heat, olive oil should be suitable in most of these recipes.

Parmesan

Parmesan is one of my favorite cheeses to use in recipes thanks to its savory, salty flavor. Note that traditional parmesan is not vegetarian because it uses animal enzymes. Look for parmesan labeled "vegetarian" if you are a strict vegetarian. I also highly recommend grating all cheeses yourself (versus buying them pre-grated, where anti-caking agents are added that can influence flavor).

Leafy Greens

I often turn to leafy greens to add a boost of veggies to a dish. Romaine is a favorite for fresh uses like salads, spinach is versatile in smoothies and cooked dishes, and kale is a go-to for adding to soups and stews.

Lentils

Lentils are a staple in vegetarian cooking, offering plenty of proteins, fiber, and essential nutrients like iron and folate. Their earthy flavor enriches soups, salads, and meatless meals, providing a satisfying, meaty texture without the meat.

Sort to remove any pebbles or bad lentils, then rinse.

Add lentils to a pot of salted water (plus desired herbs or garlic).

Cover and simmer for 20 to 30 minutes (shorter for red or yellow lentils).

1

Good Morning

Why can we eat the same breakfast virtually every morning and never get tired of it, but dinner every night must be new? As a breakfast lover who happens to be perfectly content repeating the same morning meal, this chapter takes that principle and adds...adventure.

The breakfast recipes in this book follow a choose-your-adventure model. With just a few simple base recipes, you can create dozens of unique breakfasts, kickstarting your day with nutritious flavor that adds variety to your rotation (with minimal pre-coffee cognitive function required).

In this chapter:

Have a question
about this recipe?

Avocado Toasts

Hot take: Avocado toast is not a trend and is here to stay. Because when a quick breakfast is centered around whole grains, healthy fats, and lots of flavor, it's not going anywhere. Be sure to use good bread (like a seedy whole grain or sourdough) and ripe avocados!

SERVES 1 • 10 MINUTES

Base Ingredients

2 slices toasted bread + ½ avocado + a pinch of salt and pepper

Classic Avocado Toast

½ teaspoon lemon juice

½ teaspoon extra virgin olive oil

Scoop avocado into a bowl and mash together with lemon juice, oil, salt, and pepper. Spread onto toasted bread.

Pico de Gallo Avocado Toast

¼ cup pico de gallo

Cut avocado into cubes. In a bowl, toss together avocado, pico de gallo, salt, and pepper. Spoon onto toasted bread.

Goat Cheese & Chives Avocado Toast

10 thin slices of radish

2 tablespoons crumbled goat cheese

1 tablespoon chopped chives

Scoop avocado onto toast and mash with a fork. Top with sliced radishes, goat cheese, chives, salt, and pepper.

Everything Bagel Avocado Toast

1 teaspoon everything bagel seasoning

Thinly slice avocado and arrange onto toasted bread. Sprinkle with everything bagel seasoning.

Avocado Toast with Egg

1 teaspoon olive oil

2 large eggs

Heat oil in a large saute pan over medium heat. Add the eggs and cook for 3 to 5 minutes, or until white is completely set and yolk is still a bit runny. Scoop avocado onto toast and mash with a fork, then top each piece with a cooked egg. Season with salt and pepper.

Have a question about this recipe?

Protein Toasts

Before there was avocado toast, there was just...toast. And you know what? There's something delicious about a handful of ingredients on a piece of good, toasted bread. These topping ideas balance flavor with nutrition, using protein-forward ingredients for a quick weekday kind of breakfast.

SERVES 1 • 10 MINUTES

Strawberry Yogurt Toast

1 piece of toasted bread

2 to 4 tablespoons Greek yogurt

4 strawberries (or other berries)

Optional drizzle of honey

Spread yogurt onto toasted bread. Top with sliced strawberries and optional honey.

Almond Butter Banana Toast

1 piece of toasted bread

2 tablespoons almond butter, can also use peanut butter

½ banana

Pinch of cinnamon

Spread almond butter onto toasted bread. Top with sliced banana and a pinch of cinnamon.

Blueberry Cottage Cheese Toast

1 piece of toasted bread

2 to 4 tablespoons cottage cheese

Handful of blueberries

Optional drizzle of honey

Spread cottage cheese onto toasted bread. Top with blueberries and optional honey.

Cucumber Hummus Toast

1 piece of toasted bread

2 tablespoons hummus

A few slices of cucumber

Pinch of coarse sea salt

Spread hummus onto toasted bread. Top with sliced cucumber and sea salt.

All oat recipes:

Overnight Oats

Overnight oats are the easy breakfast meal prep that dreams are made of. Add all the ingredients to a bowl or jar, seal it shut, and pop it in the fridge until morning! Come breakfast time, give it a stir and enjoy (no cooking required). The base formula makes it easy to customize the oats any way you want, and I've included 10 of our family's favorites.

SERVES 1 • 10 MINUTES HANDS-ON

Base Recipe

½ cup rolled oats

½ cup milk, can use dairy-free

1 tablespoon chia seeds

Pinch of salt

Plus desired flavor (see Flavor Options)

Assemble: In a 16-oz mason jar or bowl combine Base Recipe ingredients plus the ingredients for your desired Flavor Option. Stir to combine.

Rest: Seal shut and place in the fridge for at least 2 hours (or overnight), until oats are soft.

Serve: When ready to eat, stir then dig in! If oats look dry, add a splash of milk. You don't need to cook them, but can warm them in the microwave if desired.

Storage: Keep these in an airtight container in the fridge for up to 5 days.

Flavor Options

Brownie Batter

1 tablespoon unsweetened cocoa powder

1 tablespoon chocolate chips

1 tablespoon brown sugar

Banana Bread

1 banana, sliced

1 tablespoon brown sugar

½ teaspoon cinnamon

¼ teaspoon vanilla extract

Peaches & Cream

¼ cup chopped peaches

¼ cup plain or vanilla yogurt

1 tablespoon maple syrup

¼ teaspoon vanilla extract

Creamy Strawberry

¼ cup chopped strawberries

¼ cup plain or vanilla yogurt

1 tablespoon honey

¼ teaspoon vanilla extract

Protein Packed

¼ cup vanilla protein powder

¼ teaspoon vanilla extract

Blueberry

¼ cup blueberries, mashed

1 tablespoon honey

¼ teaspoon vanilla extract

Cookie Dough

2 tablespoons chocolate chips

1 tablespoon almond butter

1 tablespoon brown sugar

¼ teaspoon vanilla extract

Vanilla Date

4 dates, chopped

1 tablespoon honey

¼ teaspoon vanilla extract

Optionally replace table salt with flaky sea salt

Pina Colada

¼ cup chopped pineapple

1 tablespoon shredded coconut

1 tablespoon honey

¼ teaspoon vanilla extract

PB&J

2 tablespoons peanut butter or your favorite nut butter

2 tablespoons jelly

¼ teaspoon vanilla extract

All egg recipes:

Omelets

In a choose-your-adventure of omelets, I have three delicious options for you: one for when you need a basic omelet, one for when you want something fancy, and one with a pop of protein.

SERVES 1 • 20 MINUTES

The Basic Perfect Veggie Omelet

3 large eggs

2 teaspoons milk, cream, or sour cream

1 tablespoon unsalted butter, divided

¼ cup chopped mushrooms

2 tablespoons chopped white onion

2 tablespoons chopped red bell pepper

2 tablespoons chopped green bell pepper

¼ cup shredded cheddar cheese

Salt and pepper, to taste

Beat: Whisk together the eggs and dairy until smooth (the egg yolks and whites should be completely mixed together).

Veggies: Melt half of the butter in a large non-stick skillet over medium heat. Add mushrooms, onion, and peppers. Cook until soft, about 5 to 7 minutes.

Egg: Add remaining butter to the skillet and allow to melt. Reduce heat to medium/low, then pour eggs over the veggies. Allow bottom of eggs to slightly set, 2 to 3 minutes. With a spatula, gently push an edge of the egg up while tilting the pan to allow the liquidy egg on top to flow underneath. Repeat this around the edge of the pan until no liquid is left.

Cheese: When the egg is almost done cooking, sprinkle on the cheese and allow it to melt.

Fold: Fold the omelet in half or into thirds. (Pro-tip: Slide half of the omelet out of the pan and halfway onto a plate, then fold the remaining half over itself.) Season with salt and pepper. Serve immediately.

per serving: calories 368 | carbs 6.1g | fiber 1.2g | sugar 3.7g | protein 21.9g | fat 29.3g | sodium 345mg | iron 3mg

The Fancy Fluffy Soufflé Omelet

3 large eggs

¼ teaspoon salt

¼ cup shredded cheddar cheese, divided

2 tablespoons butter

Separate: Separate the egg whites from the yolks, placing them in separate bowls. Be sure to not get any drops of egg yolk in the egg whites or they won't whip correctly!

Beat Whites: In a large, clean bowl, beat the egg whites with an electric beater until you get stiff peaks.

Beat Yolks: In a separate bowl, whisk or beat together the yolk and salt until it is pale and creamy looking, about 30 seconds.

Fold: With a rubber spatula, gently fold the egg yolks into the egg whites. Add half of the cheese and fold to combine.

Cook: Melt the butter in a large non-stick skillet over medium/low heat. Add the egg mixture, using your spatula to spread it out into an even circle. Cover and cook until the bottom is golden and the top is just barely set, about 3 to 5 minutes. Sprinkle on remaining cheese, allowing it to melt.

Fold: Fold omelet in half (to do this without breaking the omelet, I like to slide the omelet halfway off the pan and onto a plate, then fold the remaining half over itself).

Serve: Season with salt and pepper. Serve immediately.

per serving: calories 532 | carbs 1.5g | fiber 0g | sugar 1.3g | protein 26.1g | fat 47.3g | sodium 1130mg | iron 3mg

The Protein Cottage Cheese Omelet

2 large eggs

1 tablespoon milk

1 teaspoon olive oil

1 cup spinach

¼ cup cottage cheese

Salt and pepper, to taste

Beat: Whisk together the eggs and milk until smooth (the egg yolks and whites should be completely mixed together).

Spinach: Add oil to a large non-stick skillet over medium heat. Add spinach, cooking until it wilts down completely, about 1 minute. Once wilted, distribute spinach evenly around the bottom of the pan.

Egg: Reduce heat to medium/low, then pour eggs over the spinach. Allow bottom of eggs to slightly set, 2 to 3 minutes. With a spatula, gently push an edge of the egg up while tilting the pan to allow the liquidy egg on top to flow underneath. Repeat this around the edge of the pan until no liquid is left.

Fold: Spoon cottage cheese onto one side of the omelet. Fold the omelet in half or into thirds. Season with salt and pepper. Serve immediately.

per serving: calories 231 | carbs 4.6g | fiber 0.7g | sugar 1.7g | protein 20.2g | fat 14.9g | sodium 384mg | iron 3mg

All smoothies:

Smoothies

My ideal day starts with a smoothie. Well, coffee. Then smoothie. But where I'll happily follow a recipe for dinner, I don't love sifting through recipes when I first wake up. So, if you're anything like me, you'll love this smoothie guide. We're walking through the basics of making a healthy smoothie from scratch so you can understand how to blitz up a tasty, wholesome breakfast with whatever you have in your kitchen! Let's blend.

SERVES 1 • 10 MINUTES

Fruit (pick 1)*

1 piece fruit (apple, pear, mango, peach, plum)

1 cup fruit (chopped pineapple, mango, berries, cherries)

Extras (choose your adventure)

1 to 2 cups leafy greens (spinach, kale, chard)

¼ cup oats (rolled or instant)

1 to 2 tablespoons protein powder

1 to 2 tablespoons seeds (chia, flax, hemp)

1 to 2 tablespoons nut butter (peanut, almond, sunflower)

1 to 2 teaspoons sweetener (honey, agave, maple syrup, Medjool date)

¼ to ½ teaspoon spices and flavorings (ginger, turmeric, cinnamon, vanilla extract)

Creamy Base (pick 1)

½ cup yogurt or kefir

½ cup cottage cheese

1 banana

½ of an avocado

Liquid

½ to 1 cup milk, juice, or coconut water

**For a frosty cold smoothie, make sure at least one fruit is frozen beforehand.*

Favorite Smoothie Recipes

Prefer something more exact? These are my all-time favorite smoothie recipes. To make smoothies in advance, place all ingredients except the liquid into a freezer-safe baggie or container. Store in the freezer. When ready to make your smoothie, empty the contents into a blender, add the liquid, and blend.

Orange Dreamsicle

1 banana, sliced and frozen
2 medium oranges, peeled
1 teaspoon of orange zest
½ cup Greek yogurt
1 teaspoon vanilla extract

Blueberry Banana

1 banana, sliced and frozen
1 cup blueberries
½ cup vanilla yogurt
½ to 1 cup milk, any variety
Optional: spoonful of nut butter, granola (for garnish)

Carrot Orange Ginger

1 banana, sliced and frozen
2 medium carrots
1 orange, peeled
1 tablespoon honey
1 teaspoon grated ginger
Liquid as needed: orange juice, coconut water, or milk

Wake Me Up

1 banana, sliced and frozen
½ cup coffee, chilled
½ cup milk, any variety
¼ cup rolled oats
Optional: spoonful of nut butter

Hidden Cauliflower

1 banana, sliced and frozen
1 cup cauliflower florets
1 cup strawberries
1 cup milk, any variety
Optional: honey

Key Lime Pie

1 banana, sliced and frozen
½ cup Greek yogurt
¼ cup key lime or lime juice
1 tablespoon honey
½ teaspoon lime zest
¼ teaspoon vanilla extract

All smoothies can be made vegan with non-dairy yogurt and milk.
Replace honey with agave or maple syrup.

Sweet Potato Black Bean Chili, page 35

2

Soupy Things

The defining feature of the recipes in this chapter is less "Soups" and more "Cozy Meals You Eat From A Bowl With A Spoon." Because between the hearty chilis, flavorful curries, and vegetable-packed stews you'll find here, relegating them to "Soup" would be a disservice.

These are some of the book's most customizable recipes because you can't mess up a soup! Add those soon-to-go-bad vegetables, throw in an extra can of beans, use whatever spices or seasonings you have - there are no rules in Soup Land.

In this chapter:

"The ultimate comfort food! So tasty! Super easy to make! My husband got 3/4s of way through dinner before he noticed there was no chicken. Officially carnivore approved!"

-Marianne

Have a question about this recipe?

Chickpeas And Dumplings

This may well be the most classic comfort food...ever? Fluffy dumplings are cooked directly in that flavorful, creamy soup (and it's all ready in under an hour). Short on time? The soup and the dumpling dough can be made up to two days ahead and then cooked together at dinner time.

SERVES 6 • 45 MINUTES

Chickpea Soup

1 tablespoon olive oil

1 cup diced yellow onion, about 1 medium onion

2 medium carrots, cut into rounds

2 stalks celery, diced

4 cloves garlic, minced

¼ cup all-purpose flour

1 teaspoon poultry seasoning

½ to 1 teaspoon salt (start with less, add more before serving if needed)

4 cups vegetable broth

1 (15-ounce) can chickpeas, drained

1 cup frozen peas

1 cup unsweetened unflavored vegan creamer*

Vegan Dumplings

2 cups all-purpose flour

1 tablespoon baking powder

1 teaspoon salt

½ teaspoon poultry seasoning

¾ cup unsweetened unflavored vegan creamer*

¼ cup olive oil

Flavor Base: Heat oil in a large pot over medium heat, then add diced onions, carrots, and celery. Cook until onion is soft, about 5 minutes. Stir in garlic and cook for another minute. Stir in flour, poultry seasoning, and salt to evenly coat veggies.

Soup: While whisking, slowly pour in the vegetable broth. Taste and add more salt if needed. Cover and bring to a gentle simmer while you prepare the dumplings.

Dumplings: Stir together flour, baking powder, salt, and poultry seasoning. Stir in vegan creamer or milk and oil, stirring just until dough comes together (do not over stir; this will result in tough dumplings).

Assemble: Add chickpeas, frozen peas, and creamer to the soup. Bring back to a simmer, then drop spoonfuls of the dumpling dough right into the soup.

Cook: Put a lid on the soup and cook for 15 minutes. Do not lift the lid while cooking. You want to build up the steam, which will cook the dumplings! After 15 minutes, check on dumplings (they should be firm, and a toothpick inserted should come out clean). Serve warm!

*You can also use evaporated milk (for non-vegan) or coconut milk.

VEGAN

per serving: calories 394 | carbs 59.7g | fiber 6.2g | sugar 5.8g | protein 9g | fat 12g | sodium 1170mg | iron 4mg

"Absolutely fabulous! The base of this soup is delicious and open to many variations. I added chopped red pepper and broccoli along with the spinach to add more veg."

-Sally

Have a question about this recipe?

Gnocchi Soup With Beans

I was a holdout on developing a gnocchi soup recipe for a long time because I thought a necessity was that it had to include either chicken or Italian sausage to be "complete." But the thing is, pillowy morsels of gnocchi speak for themselves, right? And adding creamy white beans helps.

SERVES 4 • 15 MINUTES

2 tablespoons unsalted butter

1 cup diced white or yellow onion, about 1 medium onion

½ cup diced carrots, about 1 medium carrot

½ cup diced celery, about 1 stalk

3 cloves garlic, minced

2 teaspoons Italian seasoning

1 teaspoon salt

¼ teaspoon red pepper flakes

¼ cup all-purpose flour

4 cups vegetable broth

1 (15-ounce) can white beans, drained

4 cups spinach, chopped

16 ounces gnocchi

2 cups half-and-half

Flavor Base: Melt butter in a large pot over medium heat. Add onion, carrots, and celery, cooking until onion is soft and translucent, about 5 minutes. Stir in garlic, Italian seasoning, salt, and red pepper flakes, continuing to cook for a minute. Stir in flour.

Make It Soup: While stirring, add vegetable broth and bring to a gentle simmer for 5 minutes to thicken the soup. Stir in white beans, spinach, and gnocchi, cooking just until gnocchi is tender, about 2 to 3 minutes.

Serve: Remove from heat and stir in half-and-half. Serve warm!

Level Up

Add a plant-based spicy ground sausage at the end of the 1st step, especially if you're serving meat-lovers!

per serving: calories 437 | carbs 67g | fiber 6.7g | sugar 5g | protein 15.1g | fat 7.8g | sodium 1197mg | iron 4mg

"This was delicious!!! Will definitely put on the weekly rotation! Can't wait to try more of your recipes!"

-Paula

Have a question about this recipe?

Tuscan White Bean Soup

It's difficult to call something "Tuscan" (or any region, for that matter) because it represents so much. But this soup tastes like Tuscany feels, and that's the best way I can describe it. It's got a decent amount of vegetables already, but throw in whatever wilty veggies are about to go bad in your crisper drawer!

SERVES 4 • 25 MINUTES

2 tablespoons unsalted butter

1 cup diced yellow onion, about 1 medium onion

1 cup diced carrots, about 2 medium carrots

1 cup diced celery, about 3-4 stalks

4 cloves garlic, minced

2 tablespoons tomato paste

2 tablespoons sun-dried tomatoes, finely chopped

1 tablespoon Italian seasoning

1 teaspoon each salt, red pepper flakes

4 cups vegetable broth

3 (15-ounce) cans cannellini beans, drained

2 cups chopped kale

½ cup heavy cream

½ cup grated parmesan cheese

Optional for serving: big homemade croutons, black pepper

Flavor Base: Melt butter in a large pot set over medium heat. Add onion, carrots, celery, and garlic. Cook until the onion is soft and fragrant, about 5 minutes.

Seasonings: Stir in tomato paste, sun-dried tomatoes, Italian seasoning, salt, and red pepper flakes. Continue cooking for 3 minutes.

Fillings: Stir in vegetable broth, beans, and kale. Cover and let simmer for about 10 minutes or until kale is soft.

Serve: Remove from heat and stir in cream and parmesan. Serve warm, optionally topped with croutons and fresh cracked black pepper.

Serving Tip

I love serving this soup with giant croutons! Cut large blocks of bread from a loaf of sourdough. Toss with olive oil and salt, then cook in the oven, air fryer, or stove until golden brown and crispy.

GLUTEN-FREE (omit croutons)

per serving: calories 317 | carbs 37.1g | fiber 13.2g | sugar 7g | protein 13g | fat 13.2g | sodium 1008mg | iron 3mg

SERVING TIP

I love making the croutons extra big by just tearing up a loaf of French bread, tossing in olive oil, then baking or sauteing until golden brown and crispy.

Have a question about this recipe?

Vegan Cream Of Mushroom Soup

The last thing I expected from this soup was for it to go viral on social media. Let's be honest, there's not much sexy about the words "cream of mushroom." But whether it was the umami mushrooms or the creamy blended cashew base, this recipe has been ladled into thousands of bowls (yours next?).

SERVES 4 • 30 MINUTES

1 cup raw unsalted cashews

4 tablespoons olive oil, divided

16 ounces button mushrooms, brown or white, sliced

¼ cup dry white wine

1 cup diced yellow onion, about 1 medium onion

6 cloves garlic, minced

1 tablespoon fresh thyme leaves

4 cups vegetable broth

½ teaspoon salt

¼ teaspoon ground black pepper

Optional for serving: crusty homemade croutons

Soften Cashews: Pour very hot water over cashews and let them soak while you prepare the rest of the recipe (if you don't have a strong blender, these may need to soak overnight for maximum creaminess).

Cook Mushrooms: Add 2 tablespoons of the oil to a large pot and set over medium heat. Add the mushrooms and cook until golden brown and a little crispy, about 10 minutes. Add wine to the pan, scraping the bottom of the pan with a spatula to get all the tasty flavor bits off the bottom of the pan. Cook, uncovered, until wine has evaporated out. Remove mushrooms from the pan.

Cook Aromatics: To the same pan add the 2 remaining tablespoons of oil and onion. Cook until the onion is soft and translucent, about 3 minutes. Add garlic and thyme and continuing cooking for a minute.

Blend: Add vegetable broth to the pot and stir. Ladle about half of the mixture into a standing blender. Drain cashews and add them to the blender too. Blitz until smooth and creamy, being sure to leave the lid ajar if your mixture is hot.

Assemble: Add creamy cashew mixture back into the pot along with cooked mushrooms, salt, and pepper. Let simmer, uncovered, for 15 minutes—it should thicken up a bit in this time. Taste and add more salt if needed, then serve warm.

VEGAN, GLUTEN-FREE (omit croutons)

per serving: calories 419 | carbs 20.5g | fiber 2.8g | sugar 5.9g | protein 15.5g | fat 32g | sodium 969mg | iron 4mg

"Big thumbs up for this recipe! It was a great simple dish that made plenty. Other family members really enjoyed some too which is a hard sell for the old-school ranchers! Certainly a dish I'll come back to."

-Lewis

Have a question about this recipe?

Lentil Chili

I'm a big fan of chili when it comes to feeding crowds, emptying the pantry, or having something cozy to eat on the couch. This one checks all the boxes. I like keeping the ingredients on hand (basically all pantry staples) to make a quick and flavorful dinner at the drop of a dime.

SERVES 6 • 45 MINUTES

1 tablespoon olive oil

1 cup diced white onion, about 1 medium onion

1 (1.25-ounce) packet chili seasoning

8 cups vegetable broth

1 (16-ounce) bag brown lentils

2 (14.5-ounce) cans petite diced tomatoes, do not drain

1 (15-ounce) can black beans, do not drain

Flavor Base: Heat oil in a large pot over medium heat. Add onion and cook until soft and a bit translucent, about 3 minutes. Add chili seasoning and cook for another 1 minute.

Assemble: Add broth, lentils, tomatoes, and black beans. Cover and let simmer for 25 to 30 minutes, or until lentils are tender.

Serve hot topped with your favorites like cilantro, jalapeno, avocado, and crushed corn chips!

DIY Chili Seasoning

This blend replaces one packet of store-bought chili seasoning:

2 tablespoons chili powder

2 teaspoons cumin

1 teaspoon salt

½ teaspoon each garlic powder, onion powder, ground black pepper, paprika, oregano, cocoa powder

¼ teaspoon cayenne pepper

VEGAN, GLUTEN-FREE

per serving: calories 398 | carbs 57.1g | fiber 12g | sugar 5.3g | protein 28.3g | fat 5.7g | sodium 1229mg | iron 2mg

"Really enjoyed it! I like my chili thick and chunky and this recipe did not disappoint. The 'chili meat' was especially good."

-Jon

Have a question about this recipe?

Sweet Potato Black Bean Chili

In Texas, where we spend a lot of time, chili doesn't contain beans. While I can't agree with a beanless chili, I can agree with adding a little "meat." If by meat you mean an umami-packed blend of mushrooms, walnuts, and black beans. For the "carnivores" who like meat at dinner, make this.

SERVES 4 • 50 MINUTES

Chili "Meat"

1 cup walnuts

8 ounces mushrooms

1 (15-ounce) can black beans, drained and rinsed

Chili Fillings

2 tablespoons olive oil

3 cups diced sweet potato, about 2 to 3 medium sweet potatoes

1 cup diced white onion, about 1 medium onion

4 cloves garlic, minced

2 (15-ounce) cans diced tomatoes, do not drain

1 (15-ounce) can black beans, drained and rinsed

1 ½ cups vegetable broth

Seasonings

2 tablespoons soy sauce

1 tablespoon smoked paprika

2 teaspoons cumin

1 teaspoon salt

1 teaspoon chili powder

Prep Chili "Meat": Add walnuts, mushrooms, and beans to a food processor. Blitz until mostly broken down into a chunky paste, scraping down the sides as needed.

Cook Veggies: Heat oil over medium heat in a large pot. Add sweet potato, onion, and garlic, cooking until onion is translucent and soft, about 5 minutes.

Cook "Meat": Add chili "meat" then continue to cook for 5 minutes, stirring occasionally.

Bring It Together: Add tomatoes, black beans, vegetable broth, and all seasonings.

Simmer: Cover and let simmer for 30 minutes, stirring occasionally, until consistency is thick and chili-like. (Too soupy? Let it simmer with the lid off until thick.)

Serve: Ladle into bowls, optionally topping with sour cream/yogurt, cheese, tortilla chips, or green onions.

Which mushroom is best?
Baby bella, button, and white mushrooms all work well here.

VEGAN, GLUTEN-FREE (replace soy sauce with tamari)

per serving: calories 478 | carbs 47.3g | fiber 13.1g | sugar 12.6g | protein 19.2g | fat 27.5g | sodium 1371mg | iron 5mg

"Hearty, tasty, and filling! Served with basmati rice and warm naan. This will be added to our dinner meal rotations."

-Colleen

Have a question about this recipe?

Indian-Style Lentil Curry

While I don't often create "copycat recipes," I made this recipe out of necessity. When we moved into our little Denver bungalow with a comically small pantry, I could no longer fit the Costco pouches of Madras Lentils that I had come to rely on for quick lunches and dinners. This recipe was my delicious solution.

SERVES 4 • 45 MINUTES

2 tablespoons unsalted butter

1 cup diced yellow onion, about 1 medium onion

1 red bell pepper, finely diced

4 cloves garlic, minced

2 tablespoons grated ginger

¼ cup tomato paste

2 teaspoons smoked paprika

1 teaspoon cumin

¾ teaspoon salt

½ teaspoon each ground coriander, cayenne pepper

4 cups vegetable broth

1 cup dry black lentils

1 (15-ounce) can kidney beans, drained and rinsed

½ cup half-and-half

To serve: basmati rice, cilantro, naan

Aromatics: Melt butter in a large pot over medium/high heat. Add onion, bell pepper, garlic, and ginger. Cook until onions are soft and fragrant, 3 to 5 minutes.

Flavor It Up: Stir in tomato paste, smoked paprika, cumin, salt, ground coriander, and cayenne pepper. Cook for another 3 to 5 minutes. This will transform the tomato flavor from sour to savory.

Lentils: Add vegetable broth and black lentils. Cover and let gently simmer until lentils are tender, about 25 to 30 minutes, stirring occasionally to prevent lentils from sticking to the bottom.

Rice: If serving with rice, start cooking rice now and cover to keep warm when finished.

Finishing Touches: Remove from heat and stir in kidney beans and half-and-half. Serve warm over rice, topped with cilantro, and served with naan.

Black vs. Brown Lentils

I prefer black lentils for this recipe because they hold their shape best, but brown lentils are often easier to find and work well here!

VEGAN (replace the half-and-half with coconut milk), **GLUTEN-FREE**

per serving: calories 302 | carbs 35.9g | fiber 12g | sugar 7.2g | protein 16.2g | fat 11.6g | sodium 1497mg | iron 4mg

Have a question about this recipe?

Zucchini Stew

This is the soup you make at a very specific time of year. Your zucchini plant is taking over your garden. You have more tomatoes than you know what to do with. And you absolutely, under no circumstances, want to turn on the oven. Is it soup season? Absolutely.

SERVES 4 • 45 MINUTES

1 tablespoon olive oil

3 cups chopped zucchini, about 2 medium zucchini

½ cup diced white or yellow onion, about ½ medium onion

3 cloves garlic, minced

2 cups marinara sauce

1 (15-ounce) can navy beans, drained

1 cup chopped kale

¼ cup basil, chopped

Salt and pepper, to taste

Flavor Base: Heat oil in a large pot over medium heat. Add zucchini, onion, and garlic to the pan, cooking until onion and zucchini are a bit soft, about 5 minutes.

Stewify: Stir in marinara and beans. Continue cooking, covered, for 5 minutes until hot and simmering.

Greens: Stir in kale and basil. Cook until kale wilts, about 2 minutes.

Serve: Season with salt and pepper, as needed, then serve warm!

Add Color

Use one zucchini and one yellow squash for color variation!

To make your own marinara, heat 1 tablespoon of olive oil in a large pot over medium heat. Add 3 cloves of minced garlic and cook until soft. Stir in 1 to 1 ½ pounds of fresh tomatoes and cook uncovered until tomatoes have mostly broken down, about 25 minutes, stirring often. Stir in 2 tablespoons of fresh basil, 2 tablespoons of fresh parsley, 1 tablespoon of honey, and ½ teaspoon each of salt and pepper. Continue simmering about 10 minutes.

VEGAN, GLUTEN-FREE

per serving: calories 196 | carbs 29.4g | fiber 7.1g | sugar 13.1g | protein 6g | fat 7g | sodium 682mg | iron 2mg

"Made a big pot on Saturday and was absolutely hooked after the first taste. It is absolutely perfect."

-Vik

Have a question about this recipe?

Minestrone Soup

If ever there were a choose-your-adventure of soups, it would be minestrone. Except for the mirepoix (onion, carrots, celery), everything can be improvised based on what you have. Use a different type of bean! Use a different kind of pasta! Add wilty veggies that are about to turn! There are no rules here.

SERVES 4 • 45 MINUTES

2 tablespoons olive oil

1 cup diced yellow onion, about 1 medium onion

2 medium carrots, diced

3 stalks celery, diced

4 cloves garlic, minced

1 teaspoon Italian seasoning

½ teaspoon red pepper flakes

½ to 1 teaspoon salt, start with less

2 (14.5-ounce) cans crushed tomatoes

1 (15-ounce) can kidney beans, drained and rinsed

4 cups vegetable broth

2 cups orecchiette pasta, can use any small pasta type

2 cups green beans, trimmed and chopped into bite-sizes

4 cups spinach, chopped

To serve: parmesan, crusty bread

Flavor Base: Heat oil in a large pot over medium heat. Add onion, carrots, celery, and garlic. Cook until onion and carrots soften, about 5 minutes. Stir in Italian seasoning, red pepper flakes, and salt.

Soupify: Stir in tomatoes, beans, and vegetable broth. Bring to a simmer, cover, and cook for 10 minutes.

Fillings: Add pasta and green beans, and continue cooking for 8 to 10 minutes, or until pasta is al dente. In the last minute of cooking, add the spinach, stirring until it wilts down.

Serve: Taste the soup and add remaining salt, if needed. Serve warm with your favorite bread for dipping and topped with parmesan cheese!

Thick or Thin?

This makes a thick soup. If you prefer a more liquidy soup, add 2 additional cups of broth in the 2nd step.

VEGAN (omit parmesan topping), **GLUTEN-FREE** (use gluten-free pasta)

per serving: calories 360 | carbs 54.5g | fiber 11.9g | sugar 10.6g | protein 17.6g | fat 9.5g | sodium 1607mg | iron 5mg

Have a question about this recipe?

Creamy Chickpea Kale Soup

There's a lot going for this soup - the protein-packed chickpeas, the toothy kale, that aromatic base of veggies. But my favorite thing about this soup? The smoked paprika. It gives this soup that long-simmered flavor in about half an hour.

SERVES 6 • 30 MINUTES

- 2 tablespoons unsalted butter
- 2 stalks celery, finely diced
- 2 medium carrots, finely diced
- 1 cup diced yellow onion, about 1 medium onion
- 4 cloves garlic, minced
- 2 tablespoons tomato paste
- 1 tablespoon fresh rosemary, finely chopped
- 1 teaspoon each smoked paprika and red pepper flakes
- ½ teaspoon salt
- 2 (15-ounce) cans chickpeas, drained
- 4 cups vegetable broth
- 1 cup heavy cream, can use half-and-half
- 2 cups chopped kale
- 1 tablespoon lemon juice
- To serve: parmesan cheese

Flavor Base: Melt butter in a large pan over medium heat. Add celery, carrots, onion, and garlic. Cook for 5 minutes, or until the onion is soft and translucent.

Spice It Up: Stir in tomato paste, rosemary, smoked paprika, red pepper flakes, and salt. Continue cooking for 3 minutes, stirring occasionally.

Cook: Add chickpeas and vegetable broth. Cover and simmer for 10 minutes.

Finish: Remove from heat, then stir in cream and kale. Stir until the kale is completely submerged and wilted, about a minute. Stir in lemon juice and serve hot, optionally topping each bowl with freshly grated parmesan!

VEGAN (use vegan butter and coconut milk instead of cream), **GLUTEN-FREE**

per serving: calories 469 | carbs 56.2g | fiber 11.2g | sugar 5.3g | protein 17g | fat 20.7g | sodium 1714mg | iron 4mg

SWAP THE BEANS

You can sub one or both cans of cannellini for navy or Great Northern beans.

Have a question about this recipe?

White Bean Chili

The destination: a classic recipe reminiscent of white chicken chili. The road to get there: anything but usual. Tempeh creates the ground "meat" base, and sauerkraut finishes it off with a punch of salty acidity. And we'll mash the beans so we can omit the cream altogether. A family-favorite!

SERVES 4 • 30 MINUTES

1 (8-ounce) package tempeh

1 tablespoon olive oil

1 cup diced white or yellow onion, about 1 medium onion

4 cloves garlic, minced

1 teaspoon each cumin, ground coriander, oregano

½ teaspoon each salt, white pepper

2 (15-ounce) cans cannellini beans, drained

1 (15-ounce) can chickpeas, drained

4 cups vegetable broth

2 cups sauerkraut

¼ cup cilantro, chopped

2 tablespoons lime juice

To serve: shredded white cheddar cheese, plain Greek yogurt or sour cream

Prep Tempeh: Using a box grater, roughly grate the tempeh.

Flavor Base: Heat oil in a large pot over medium heat. Add onion and garlic, cooking until onion is slightly soft and translucent, about 3 minutes.

Cook Tempeh: Add the grated tempeh, cumin, coriander, oregano, salt, and pepper. Cook until tempeh is lightly browned, about 5 minutes.

Beans: Scooch tempeh mixture to one side of the pot. Add the beans and chickpeas to the empty side of the pot. Using a potato masher or fork, roughly mash about a third of the beans.

Soupify: Add broth and sauerkraut. Bring to a simmer for 5 minutes. Right before serving, mix in cilantro and lime juice. Serve hot, topped with grated white cheddar cheese and a dollop of Greek yogurt.

Probiotic Tip

I add the sauerkraut during cooking to infuse the most flavor into the soup, but adding it at the end preserves more probiotics. Your pick!

VEGAN (replace dairy toppings with sliced avocado), **GLUTEN-FREE** (check tempeh packaging)

per serving: calories 367 | carbs 44.8g | fiber 10.7g | sugar 3.2g | protein 25.7g | fat 12g | sodium 1966mg | iron 6mg

"Super easy, delicious, and healthy...that's the trifecta of perfection! This can easily be made on a busy weeknight. And the aroma as it cooks is mouth-watering."

-Miyako

Have a question about this recipe?

Coconut Kidney Bean Curry

This is the recipe whose ingredients you keep in your pantry for when you're craving a takeout-level meal. With heaps of flavor (and finished cooking in less time than delivery takes), you'll thank yourself later for stocking up on the ingredients to make this one!

SERVES 3 to 4 • 30 MINUTES

1 tablespoon olive oil

1 cup diced white onion, about 1 medium onion

2 cloves garlic, minced

2 tablespoons grated ginger

1 tablespoon garam masala

1 (15-ounce) can crushed tomatoes

1 (13-ounce) can full-fat coconut milk

1 (15-ounce) can kidney beans, drained and rinsed

2 teaspoons soy sauce

½ teaspoon salt

To serve: basmati rice, cilantro, crushed red pepper flakes, lime juice

Rice: If serving with rice, start cooking rice now and cover to keep warm when finished.

Flavor Makers: Heat oil in a large pot over medium heat. Add onion, cooking until very soft, about 10 minutes. Add garlic, ginger, and garam masala and cook for another minute.

Filler Uppers: Add tomatoes, coconut milk, kidney beans, soy sauce, and salt, then bring to a gentle simmer. Cover and simmer for 10 minutes to let flavors blend together, stirring occassionally.

Serve: Ladle curry over warm rice. Top with cilantro, a pinch of crushed red pepper, and a squeeze of lime juice.

DIY *Garam Masala*

You can make your own with this simple garam masala blend:

1 tablespoon ground cumin

1 tablespoon ground coriander

2 teaspoons ground cardamom

1 teaspoon ground cinnamon

1 teaspoon ground black pepper

½ teaspoon ground cloves

¼ teaspoon ground nutmeg

VEGAN, GLUTEN-FREE (replace soy sauce with tamari)

per serving: calories 386 | carbs 34.8g | fiber 10.2g | sugar 9.1g | protein 10.8g | fat 23.4g | sodium 1063mg | iron 3mg (assuming 3 servings)

"I just made this recipe for lunch today, and everybody loved it! I wanted to put a straw in the broth, and just drink it as fast as possible! Very flavorful, and healthy!"

-Silvana

Have a question about this recipe?

Thai Coconut Curry With Tofu

Lifelong peanut and shellfish allergies gave me an unfounded fear of Thai food well into adulthood. But after learning how to make Thai curries at a cooking school in Chiang Mai, it was like seeing color for the first time. This recipe is my take on a classic Thai curry (with ingredients found at most grocery stores).

SERVES 4 • 45 MINUTES

Curry

1 tablespoon coconut oil

2 tablespoons chopped shallots, about 1 small shallot

1 tablespoon grated ginger

2 tablespoons Thai red curry paste

2 (13-ounce) cans full-fat coconut milk

1 teaspoon vegetable bouillon (just bouillion, no water)

2 tablespoons soy sauce

2 tablespoons honey

1 tablespoon chili garlic sauce

Fillings

1 cup dry rice or 4 ounces rice noodles

1 (14-ounce) block firm or extra firm tofu

1 tablespoon coconut oil

1 cup shredded or sliced carrots

1 cup thinly sliced red cabbage

1 cup snap peas

Curry: Heat oil in a large saute pan or wok over medium heat. Add shallots and ginger, cooking for 2 to 3 minutes until shallots are translucent. Add curry paste and cook for 1 more minute, until fragrant. Add coconut milk, bouillon, soy sauce, honey, and chili garlic sauce. Cover and let simmer while you prepare the rest.

Starch: Prepare rice or rice noodles according to instructions on package.

Tofu: Drain and pat tofu as dry as possible with paper towels. Cut into bite-sized cubes. Heat oil in a large saute pan or wok over medium/high heat, then add the tofu. Cook until sides are slightly browned, then add in a few spoonfuls of your curry. Cook for a minute or two, until curry has evaporated, then remove tofu from pan.

Veggies: Add carrots, cabbage, and snap peas to the pan the tofu was just in and cook over medium/high heat until colors are vibrant, about 3 minutes.

Serve: Combine curry, tofu, and vegetables in a pan, or assemble in individual bowls, serving with prepared rice or noodles.

Great for Meal Prep

Make a batch and portion into containers for the week, storing curry separately from the rice until ready to enjoy.

VEGAN (replace honey with sugar or agave), **GLUTEN-FREE** (replace soy sauce with tamari)

per serving (with rice): calories 426 | carbs 41.7g | fiber 4.6g | sugar 14.3g | protein 14.8g | fat 23.3g | sodium 1107mg | iron 4mg

Smashed Brussels Sprouts, page 68

3

Salads & Sides

This book is all about quickly getting easy vegetarian meals onto your plate, and these flavorful sides fit the bill. Many are suitable for meal prep, meaning you can make them a few days in advance for leisurely lunch or dinner sides throughout the week.

In this chapter:

salads & sides

Zucchini Corn Salad

SERVES 4 to 6 • 25 MINUTES • MEAL PREP UP TO 5 DAYS

½ cup extra virgin olive oil

2 cloves garlic, minced

½ teaspoon each salt and pepper

¼ teaspoon red pepper flakes

2 ears corn

4 medium zucchini, cut in half lengthwise

4 teaspoons lemon juice

4 to 8 ounces feta cheese, crumbled (amount to your liking)

Oil: Combine oil, garlic, and spices. Brush corn and zucchini with ¼ cup of the mixture (set aside the rest).

Option 1 - Grill: Grill veggies over medium/high heat, flipping occasionally to evenly cook, and charring some for flavor. Zucchini is done when soft, about 10 minutes. Corn may take a little longer, about 15 minutes, and is done when bright yellow.

Option 2 - Oven: Preheat oven to 425°F. Wrap each corn in aluminum foil. Place corn and zucchini on a baking sheet and bake for 25 to 30 minutes, flipping during cooking, until zucchini is soft and corn is bright yellow. Turn your oven to “broil” (about 550°F). Unwrap corn, and return tray to the oven. Cook for just 2 to 3 minutes, watching closely until a little char develops.

Cut: Cut corn from cob. Cut zucchini into bite-sizes.

Assemble: Whisk lemon juice into remaining oil mixture. Stir in grilled veggies and feta cheese.

VEGAN (omit feta), **GLUTEN-FREE**

per serving: calories 192 | carbs 11g | fiber 2g | sugar 3g | protein 4g | fat 16g | sodium 319mg | iron 1.4mg (assuming 4 servings)

Have a question about this recipe?

salads & sides

Israeli Sunshine Salad

SERVES 4 • 15 MINUTES • MEAL PREP UP TO 7 DAYS

2 limes

1 teaspoon salt

¼ cup tahini

¼ cup extra virgin olive oil

1 (15-ounce) can chickpeas, drained

2 medium cucumbers, cut into bite-sized pieces

5 stalks celery, diced

½ cup cilantro, finely chopped

Dressing: Grate the zest from 1 lime and add it to a medium bowl, along with the juice from both limes. Whisk in salt, tahini, and olive oil.

Salad: To a large bowl add chickpeas, cucumber, celery, and cilantro.

Toss: Drizzle the dressing over the salad and toss to combine. Serve immediately or store in an airtight container in the fridge.

Reader Recipe

This recipe came to me from a reader, Rudy, during Reader Recipe Week! He said, "I was inspired by the 'Israeli Salad' I had in a California cafe ten years ago. I recreated it from forgotten memory. Poor memory but good salad!".

VEGAN, GLUTEN-FREE

per serving: calories 327 | carbs 30.5g | fiber 6.9g | sugar 3.5g | protein 7.8g | fat 21.8g | sodium 853mg | iron 3mg

Have a question about this recipe?

salads & sides

Summer Veggie Salad

SERVES 4 • 15 MINUTES • MEAL PREP UP TO 5 DAYS

Dressing

2 tablespoons extra virgin olive oil

¼ cup Italian (flat-leaf) parsley, thick stems removed then chopped

1 teaspoon lemon juice

½ teaspoon oregano

1 clove garlic, minced

Pinch of salt and pepper

Salad

2 tomatoes, about 1 cup diced

½ medium cucumber, diced

1 red bell pepper, diced

½ cup diced red onion, about ½ medium onion

½ cup cubed feta cheese

Dressing: Whisk together the Dressing ingredients.

Salad: Chop all Salad ingredients into equal-sized chunks. Toss together in a large bowl.

Assemble: Add the dressing to the salad, tossing to evenly coat. For tastiest results, let chill in the refrigerator for 1 hour prior to serving.

VEGAN (omit feta), **GLUTEN-FREE**

per serving: calories 147 | carbs 9.4g | fiber 1.9g | sugar 5.9g | protein 4.1g | fat 11.3g | sodium 256mg | iron 1mg

Have a question about this recipe?

salads & sides

Mexican Street Corn Salad

SERVES 6 to 8 • 25 MINUTES • MEAL PREP UP TO 5 DAYS

Dressing

½ cup plain nonfat yogurt

1 tablespoon lime juice

1 teaspoon honey

½ teaspoon paprika

¼ teaspoon cumin

Salad

1 tablespoon olive oil

3 cups corn, from 4 ears or 2 (15-ounce) cans

1 clove garlic, minced

2 tablespoons lime juice

¼ teaspoon salt

1 (15-ounce) can black beans, drained and rinsed

1 red bell pepper, chopped

½ cup diced red onion, about ½ medium onion

½ cup crumbled cotija cheese, can substitute feta

½ cup cilantro, chopped

Dressing: Mix all Dressing ingredients together and set aside.

Cook Corn: Heat oil in a large saute pan over medium heat then add corn and garlic. Cook about 15 minutes, stirring frequently, until corn begins to char a bit. Toss with lime juice and salt.

Serve: In a large bowl, combine cooked corn, black beans, bell pepper, onion, cheese, cilantro, and dressing. Serve warm or cold. Great on tacos, as a chip dip, or by itself!

GLUTEN-FREE

per serving: calories 181 | carbs 28.6g | fiber 5.8g | sugar 3.3g | protein 8.8g | fat 4.6g | sodium 192mg | iron 1mg (assuming 8 servings)

Have a question about this recipe?

salads & sides

Chickpea Corn Salad

SERVES 4 • 15 MINUTES • MEAL PREP UP TO 5 DAYS

Dressing

½ cup plain Greek yogurt

1 tablespoon lime juice

½ teaspoon smoked paprika

¼ teaspoon each cumin, salt, pepper

1 clove garlic, minced

Salad

1 (15-ounce) can corn, drained

1 (15-ounce) can chickpeas, drained

1 red bell pepper, chopped

¼ cup diced red onion, about ¼ medium onion

½ cup chopped green onions

½ cup Italian (flat-leaf) parsley, thick stems removed then chopped

½ cup crumbled feta cheese

Dressing: In a large bowl, mix together all Dressing ingredients.

Salad: In a separate bowl, toss together all Salad ingredients

Assemble: Drizzle dressing over salad and toss to evenly combine. Serve at room temperature or chilled.

GLUTEN-FREE

per serving: calories 287 | carbs 39.5g | fiber 6.8g | sugar 6.9g | protein 11.1g | fat 11.2g | sodium 661mg | iron 3.8mg

salads & sides

Thai Cucumber Salad

SERVES 4 • 15 MINUTES • MEAL PREP UP TO 7 DAYS

Dressing

¼ cup rice vinegar

2 tablespoons sugar

1 teaspoon toasted sesame oil

¼ teaspoon each salt, red pepper flakes

2 cloves garlic, minced

Salad

2 English cucumbers

4 green onions

¼ cup cilantro

Optional: handful of chopped peanuts or almonds

Dressing: Whisk together all Dressing ingredients to dissolve the sugar.

Salad: Slice cucumbers into ¼-inch rounds. Thinly slice the green onions. Finely chop the cilantro. Toss it all together, optionally adding a handful of chopped peanuts or almonds.

Assemble: Drizzle dressing over cucumber salad and toss combine.

VEGAN, GLUTEN-FREE

per serving: calories 87 | carbs 19.2g | fiber 1.2g | sugar 15.5g | protein 1.3g | fat 0.2g | sodium 153mg | iron 1mg

Have a question about this recipe?

salads & sides

Tabbouleh Salad

SERVES 8 to 10 • 30 MINUTES • MEAL PREP UP TO 5 DAYS

- ½ cup bulgur*
- 1 cup water
- 1 cup diced cucumber, about ½ medium cucumber
- 1 cup diced fresh tomato, any variety
- 1 teaspoon salt, divided
- 3 cups Italian (flat-leaf) parsley, thick stems removed then finely chopped
- ¼ cup mint leaves, finely chopped
- 2 green onions, thinly sliced
- ¼ cup extra virgin olive oil
- 3 tablespoons lemon juice
- 1 clove garlic, minced

*Make it gluten-free by using the same amount of quinoa instead of bulgur, which contains gluten.

Cook Bulgur: Bring bulgur and water to a boil in a small pot, then cover and simmer for 15 to 20 minutes, or until tender. Allow bulgur to cool slightly.

Prep Veggies: Meanwhile, stir together cucumber, tomato, and ½ teaspoon salt. Place in a colander to allow excess moisture to drain out. Let drain for 10 minutes (or until the rest of the recipe is ready).

Chop: Remove the thick stems from the parsley and mint, then finely chop. Slice the green onion.

Dressing: Whisk together olive oil, lemon juice, garlic, and remaining ½ teaspoon of salt.

Assemble: In a large bowl, toss together cooled bulgur, strained cucumber and tomato, herbs, green onion, and dressing.

VEGAN, GLUTEN-FREE (see notes)

per serving: calories 69 | carbs 7.1g | fiber 2.1g | sugar 0.9g | protein 1.5g | fat 4.5g | sodium 205mg | iron 1mg (assuming 10 servings)

Have a question about this recipe?

salads & sides

Mexican Bean Salad

SERVES 6 • 15 MINUTES • MEAL PREP UP TO 7 DAYS

Dressing

½ cup white vinegar

¼ cup olive oil

1 tablespoon sugar

2 teaspoons ground cumin

½ teaspoon salt

¼ teaspoon ground black pepper

Salad

2 (15-ounce) cans pinto or kidney beans, drained and rinsed

1 (15-ounce) can black beans, drained and rinsed

1 (15-ounce) can corn, drained

1 red bell pepper, diced

½ cup diced red onion, about ½ medium onion

2 jalapenos, deseeded and finely chopped

¼ cup cilantro, chopped

Dressing: Whisk together all Dressing ingredients.

Salad: Toss together the Salad ingredients.

Combine: Mix the dressing into the salad mixture. Cover and refrigerate for an hour to allow flavors to mix (can skip this step if necessary).

Serving Ideas: This can be enjoyed as a side salad, chip dip, a salad topper, burrito stuffer—we eat it with everything!

VEGAN, GLUTEN-FREE

per serving: calories 100 | carbs 11.2g | fiber 2.8g | sugar 2.6g | protein 2.8g | fat 5.1g | sodium 314mg | iron 1.3mg

salads & sides

Mediterranean Parsley Salad

SERVES 4 • 15 MINUTES

Dressing

¼ cup extra virgin olive oil

2 tablespoons lemon juice

1 teaspoon lemon zest

1 teaspoon Dijon mustard

¼ teaspoon each salt and pepper

2 cloves garlic, minced

Salad

4 cups Italian (flat-leaf) parsley, thick stems removed

1 cup sliced cucumber

1 cup chopped tomato, any variety

½ medium red onion, sliced

½ cup cubed feta cheese

Dressing: Whisk together all Dressing ingredients.

Salad: Wash and chop all Salad ingredients, then transfer to a large mixing bowl.

Combine: Drizzle dressing over salad then gently toss together.

Meal prep: It's best to store the dressing and salad separately if making this ahead, although the parsley stands up better to storage than most other leafy greens! Will keep in the fridge for about 3 days.

Curly vs. Italian

Curly parsley has less flavor and is typically used as a garnish, whereas Italian (or flat-leafed) parsley has more flavor and is used as an ingredient in recipes.

GLUTEN-FREE

per serving: calories 172 | carbs 8.6g | fiber 3.1g | sugar 2.9g | protein 4g | fat 15.1g | sodium 293mg | iron 4mg

Have a question about this recipe?

salads & sides

Cottage Cheese Salad

SERVES 6 • 15 MINUTES

Sunshiney Vegetables

12 ounces cherry tomatoes, halved

½ of an English cucumber, sliced

4 green onions (whites and greens separated), sliced

½ teaspoon salt

1 tablespoon extra virgin olive oil

1 tablespoon lemon juice

Pinch black pepper

Herby Cottage Cheese

1 (16-ounce) container large curd cottage cheese

1 tablespoon lemon juice

1 teaspoon fresh dill, finely chopped

¼ teaspoon salt

Mix Veggies: In a large bowl, toss together tomatoes, cucumber, just the white parts of the green onions, and salt. Set aside.

Cottage Cheese: Combine all of the Herby Cottage Cheese ingredients in a separate bowl.

Finish Veggies: Tilt the bowl with the veggies to pour out excess juices. Stir in the olive oil, lemon juice, and pepper.

Assemble: Spoon cottage cheese mixture onto a serving platter and spread into an even layer. Spoon mixed veggies on top. Sprinkle with the green parts of the green onion. Serve fresh with crusty bread.

Meal prep: Keep the veggies and the cottage cheese mixture separate until ready to serve. Will keep in the fridge for up to 5 days.

GLUTEN-FREE

per serving: calories 99 | carbs 6g | fiber 1.1g | sugar 4.2g | protein 7.4g | fat 5g | sodium 532mg | iron 0mg

salads & sides

Panzanella Toscana

SERVES 8 • 30 MINUTES

Salad

1 pound French bread, cubed

¼ cup extra virgin olive oil

2 pounds tomatoes, any variety

1 teaspoon salt

1 yellow bell pepper, chopped

1 red bell pepper, chopped

1 cucumber, chopped

½ medium red onion, sliced

1 cup basil, chopped

Dressing

¼ cup extra virgin olive oil

3 cloves garlic, minced

2 tablespoons red wine vinegar

½ teaspoon Dijon mustard

Bread: Preheat oven to 350°F. Combine cubed bread and olive oil in a large bowl, using your hands to work the oil evenly around the cubes. Transfer to a baking sheet and bake for 20 to 30 minutes, or until crisp to the touch (but not browned).

Drain Tomatoes: Cut tomatoes into bite-sized pieces. Set a colander over a bowl and place tomatoes in the colander. Sprinkle with salt and stir to combine, then let tomatoes sit and drain until bread is finished. Reserve the juices that drip out.

Salad: In a large bowl, combine cooked bread, drained tomatoes, bell peppers, cucumber, onion, and basil.

Dressing: Whisk together the juice from the drained tomatoes and all other Dressing ingredients. Drizzle over the bread mixture, tossing to coat.

VEGAN, GLUTEN-FREE (use gluten-free bread)

per serving: calories 314 | carbs 41.2g | fiber 3.5g | sugar 6.9g | protein 8.5g | fat 14g | sodium 671mg | iron 3mg

Have a question about this recipe?

Level it up! Stir in some roasted chickpeas and roll it all in a tortilla wrap for an easy lunch!

salads & sides

Vegetarian Caesar Salad

SERVES 4 • 15 MINUTES

Dressing

½ cup extra virgin olive oil

¼ cup mayonnaise

¼ cup shaved parmesan cheese

2 tablespoons lemon juice

1 ½ teaspoon Dijon mustard

1 clove garlic

Salt and pepper, to taste

Salad

5 heaping cups chopped romaine or mixed greens

2 cups croutons

½ cup shaved parmesan cheese

Dressing: Add all Dressing ingredients to a blender and blitz until smooth and creamy. Taste and add salt and pepper as needed.

Salad: Roughly chop romaine or mixed greens. Toss together with croutons and parmesan. Drizzle with dressing and toss to coat (you may not need all of the dressing).

DIY Croutons

Mix 2 cups of cut or torn up bread, 2 tablespoons of olive oil, and ¼ teaspoon salt. Cook on the stove (medium heat) or in the air fryer or oven (400°F) until brown and crispy.

GLUTEN-FREE (use gluten-free croutons)

per serving: calories 409 | carbs 16.9g | fiber 1.7g | sugar 1.3g | protein 8.9g | fat 35.5g | sodium 516mg | iron 1.8mg

"It's incredible how good the dressing is, with the tahini, lemon juice, and plain Greek yogurt perfectly balancing the kale's bitterness. I ended up making this recipe twice in not even a month!"

-Evelyne

Have a question about this recipe?

Crunchy Kale Chickpea Salad

Tahini is the key to this powerhouse salad, which is more a main dish than a side. We'll first use that creamy sesame paste to create a crunchy coating on the chickpeas. While those roast, whisk together the lemony tahini dressing. The result is an explosion of textures and flavors—there won't be leftovers!

SERVES 4 • 30 MINUTES

Crunchy Chickpeas

1 (15-ounce) can chickpeas, drained

¼ cup tahini

½ teaspoon each salt, onion powder, garlic powder, smoked paprika

Tahini Dressing

½ cup plain Greek yogurt

¼ cup tahini

2 tablespoons lemon juice

2 teaspoons Dijon mustard

1 clove garlic, minced

½ teaspoon salt

Water as needed to thin

Salad

1 bunch kale

1 cup grated parmesan cheese

Prep Chickpeas: Preheat oven to 400°F. In a medium bowl, stir together chickpeas, tahini, and seasonings.

Bake Chickpeas: Spread chickpeas onto a parchment-lined baking sheet in a single layer, then bake for about 20 minutes, or until crispy.

Dressing: While chickpeas cook, stir together all Tahini Dressing ingredients, adding water to thin to your desired consistency.

Assemble: Wash then cut kale into bite-sized pieces, removing the tough stems. Add to a large bowl and gently massage the kale for a few seconds to make it more tender. Add Crunchy Chickpeas, Tahini Dressing, and parmesan. Toss to combine and serve!

Why massage kale?

This step helps to tenderize this hardy green, making it easier to chew and digest.

VEGAN (use a dairy-free yogurt and omit parmesan), **GLUTEN-FREE**

per serving: calories 411 | carbs 33.7g | fiber 7.6g | sugar 1.3g | protein 22.2g | fat 21.5g | sodium 1100mg | iron 5mg

> *"This was a delicious, easy meal! My kids kept asking for more! I put leftovers in a wrap for lunch the next day."*
>
> *-Becky*

Have a question about this recipe?

Mediterranean Roasted Veggies

Are you tired of bland veggies? These roasted vegetables take things up a few notches with strong seasoning and dill yogurt sauce. Love at first bite!

SERVES 4 to 6 • 45 MINUTES

Mediterranean Vegetables

1 small head cauliflower, cut into small florets

1 (15-ounce) can chickpeas, drained

1 red bell pepper, chopped

2 medium zucchini, chopped

3 medium carrots, chopped

1 medium red onion, sliced

¼ cup olive oil

1 teaspoon each oregano, dried thyme, garlic powder

¼ teaspoon each salt and pepper

Yogurt Dill Sauce

1 cup plain Greek yogurt

4 cloves garlic, minced

¼ cup dill, finely chopped

2 tablespoons lemon juice

Pinch each salt and pepper

Water to thin

Prep: Preheat oven to 425°F. Cut veggies into bite-sized pieces. In a large bowl, toss together all veggies, oil, and spices.

Bake: Spread into a single layer onto an unlined baking sheet. Bake for 20 to 30 minutes, or until cauliflower is fork-tender and chickpeas are a bit crispy.

Sauce: While veggies cook, stir together all ingredients for the Yogurt Dill Sauce, adding water to thin to your desired consistency.

Serve: Serve warm with sauce!

Meal prep: Good in the fridge for 5 to 7 days (keep veggies and sauce separate until serving).

VEGAN (use a dairy-free yogurt), **GLUTEN-FREE**

per serving: calories 343 | carbs 42.5g | fiber 8.7g | sugar 15.4g | protein 9.9g | fat 17g | sodium 443mg | iron 4mg

Smashed Veggies

In the first Live Eat Learn cookbook, I had to include our most viral recipe series ever—SMASHED VEGGIES. The concept is simple: Precook your veggies until they're tender, smash them, flavor them, and bake until crispy. Smashing helps to release moisture from the veggies so they can become crispier. It also creates more surface area for browning (and browning = flavor).

The path to smashed veggies is anything but formulaic, so pick an ingredient, method, and flavor that suits you and get to smashing!

SERVES 4 • 30 to 60 MINUTES

Step 1. Choose Your Ingredient

Brussels Sprouts (1 pound) - halve them if they're large

Cauliflower (1 large head) - cut into florets

Carrots (1 pound) - cut into bite-sized pieces or use baby carrots

Broccoli (2 heads) - cut into florets

Potatoes (1 pound) - use small potatoes or cut large potatoes into chunks

Radishes (1 pound) - halve them if they're large

Step 2. Choose Your Precook Method

Steam: Add veggies to a steamer basket placed over boiling water, cover, and steam until fork tender (about 5 minutes for tender veggies, 20 minutes for firmer veggies).

Boil: Add veggies to a pot of boiling water and cook until tender (about 3 minutes for tender veggies, 10 minutes for firmer veggies).

Microwave: Add the veggies to a microwave-safe bowl along with a splash of water. Cover with a plate (or plastic wrap) and cook on high until tender (about 4 minutes for tender veggies, 8 minutes for firmer veggies).

Bake: Spread veggies onto a baking sheet, drizzle with a bit of oil, and bake at 400°F until tender (about 15 minutes for tender veggies, 30 minutes for firmer veggies).

Step 3. SMASH!

Once your vegetables are tender, place them on a parchment-lined baking sheet in a single layer. Use a cup to firmly smash each piece until flattened.

Step 4. Brush With Oil

Brush each flattened veggie with oil to help it brown in the final cooking stage. You should need about 1 to 2 tablespoons.

Step 5. Choose Your Flavor

Now that you've maximized that surface area, they're ready to be flavored! Choose your flavoring and sprinkle or brush it evenly over the smashed veggies.

Garlic Lemon Parmesan: 4 cloves garlic (minced) mixed with ½ cup grated parmesan, ½ teaspoon salt, and the juice and zest from 1 lemon

Lemon Pepper: 1 tablespoon lemon pepper seasoning

Ranch: 2 tablespoons ranch seasoning mix with ½ cup grated parmesan

Pesto: 2 tablespoons pesto mixed with ¼ cup grated parmesan

Nooch: ¼ cup nutritional yeast mixed with 1 teaspoon salt and ½ teaspoon black pepper

Step 6. Bake

Bake at 400°F for 10 to 20 minutes or until veggies are brown and crispy at the edges.

Vegan Sloppy Joes, page 81

4

Sandwiches & Wraps

For most people, a sandwich isn't complete without meat. And for much of my life, I thought vegetarian sandwiches and wraps were just too dull to be worth putting out into the world.

And that's why you won't find the classic white bread / sad lunch sandwich here. This is a collection of hearty hot sandwiches and dinner-worthy wraps (along with tacos and burgers, because aren't those technically sandwiches, too?).

As with most of this book, these are geared toward dinner, though most also make a great midday meal!

In this chapter:

"This is one of my go-to vegetarian meals. It's so easy to put together. If I'm feeling particularly lazy (or exhausted) I just pick up a premade tzakziki sauce at my local grocery store, super delicious! Thank you for this recipe."

-Sarah

Have a question about this recipe?

Roasted Chickpea Gyros

I couldn't not include this recipe in my first real cookbook—it's the one that put me on the map. Crispy spiced chickpeas topped with creamy tzatziki sauce wrapped in pillowy pita bread. Throw all the components into bowls and everyone at the table can build their own!

SERVES 4 • 30 MINUTES

Roasted Chickpeas

1 (15-ounce) can chickpeas, drained

1 tablespoon olive oil

1 tablespoon smoked paprika

1 teaspoon ground black pepper

¼ teaspoon cayenne pepper*

¼ teaspoon salt

Tzatziki

1 cup plain Greek yogurt

½ cup shredded or diced cucumber

1 tablespoon lemon juice or vinegar

1 clove garlic, minced

1 teaspoon chopped fresh dill

¼ teaspoon each salt and pepper

To serve

4 pita flatbreads

¼ medium red onion, sliced

2 lettuce leaves, roughly chopped

1 tomato, sliced

*These gyros are spicy. If you don't like spicy foods, halve the amount of black pepper and cayenne pepper. Taste a chickpea before baking and adjust flavors as needed.

Prep: Preheat oven to 400°F. Pat dry chickpeas with a paper towel. Toss chickpeas with oil, paprika, black pepper, cayenne pepper, and salt.

Roast: Spread chickpeas onto a rimmed baking sheet and roast for about 20 minutes, until lightly browned and crispy.

Tzatziki: While chickpeas roast, stir together all Tzatziki ingredients.

Assemble: Spread tzatziki onto one side of the pita, then sprinkle in a quarter of the chickpeas and desired veggies.

If your pita breads crack when you fold them, cover them with a moist paper towel and microwave for 20 seconds. Assemble your sandwich immediately after microwaving.

Great for Meal Prep!

VEGAN (use vegan yogurt), **GLUTEN-FREE** (use gluten-free wraps)

per serving: calories 331 | carbs 45g | fiber 7.5g | sugar 6.3g | protein 11.5g | fat 12.6g | sodium 575mg | iron 4mg

"Just made this for my vegetarian son. He used to love a tuna salad sandwich. This is so good, he loved it. This recipe is going in our regular rotation. I added a bit more caper than called for but otherwise followed recipe exactly. It was delicious!"

-Mary

Have a question about this recipe?

Chickpea Tuna Melt

Is there anything a can of chickpeas can't become? Plant-based fish recipes are some of my favorites to develop because you just throw all the flavors of the ocean in (sans fish). Capers carry the weight here, and if you have nori in the back of your pantry, crumble it up and throw it in for even more fishy flavor!

SERVES 2 • 20 MINUTES

Tuna Salad

1 (15-ounce) can chickpeas, drained

¼ cup finely chopped red onion, about ¼ of a medium onion

¼ cup finely chopped celery, about ½ a stalk

1 teaspoon capers, finely chopped

¼ cup mayonnaise

2 teaspoons white vinegar

1 teaspoon Dijon mustard

Salt and pepper, to taste

Sandwich Fixings

1 tablespoon mayonnaise

4 slices sourdough bread

4 slices tomato

2 slices sharp cheddar, provolone, or American cheese

Tuna Salad: Roughly smash the chickpeas with a fork or your fingers. Stir all Tuna Salad ingredients together, adding a pinch of salt and pepper as needed to suit your taste.

Assemble Sandwich: Spread mayonnaise onto one side of each slice of bread (this replaces the butter on the outside of the sandwich, creating a golden brown crispy crust when cooked!). On the mayo-free side, layer in the tuna salad, tomato, and cheese.

Cook: Cook sandwiches over medium heat in a large skillet or panini press until outsides are golden brown and cheese has melted.

VEGAN (use vegan mayo and cheese), **GLUTEN-FREE** (use gluten-free bread)

per serving: calories 668 | carbs 88.3g | fiber 10.2g | sugar 5.3g | protein 24.3g | fat 25g | sodium 1468mg | iron 5mg

"Invited my meat eater friends over for pulled pork sliders. After a couple of servings someone asked "I thought you didn't eat meat?" I responded...I don't but I eat mushrooms!"

-Diane

Have a question about this recipe?

BBQ Pulled Mushrooms

By shredding king oyster mushrooms, seasoning, and baking, you can create a vegan pulled pork that rivals the real stuff! It's the perfect pulled pork alternative for sandwiches, tacos, nachos - the world is your oyster (mushroom). My go-to spot for finding king oysters is always a local Asian supermarket.

SERVES 2 • 30 MINUTES

- 4 king oyster mushrooms
- 2 tablespoons olive oil, divided
- 1 teaspoon smoked paprika
- ¼ teaspoon each salt, cayenne pepper
- 2 cloves garlic, minced
- ¼ cup BBQ sauce
- Recommended for serving: burger buns

Shred Mushrooms: Preheat oven to 400°F. Clean mushrooms with a damp paper towel. Using two forks, shred the stems and caps roughly into pieces. Set on a parchment-lined baking sheet.

Bake: Drizzle with 1 tablespoon of the oil, paprika, salt, cayenne, and garlic. Toss around to evenly coat the mushrooms, then bake for 20 minutes, or until mushrooms are a bit crispy and brown at the edges.

Saute: Heat remaining 1 tablespoon oil in a large saute pan over medium/high heat. Transfer cooked mushrooms to pan and add BBQ sauce. Stir and cook for 3 to 5 minutes, until mixture is thick and fragrant. Serve warm on sandwiches, nachos, salads, tacos... or however you would eat pulled pork!

1

2

3

Mushroom Varieties

You can use regular oyster mushrooms if you can't find king oysters, though you will need more (about 3 heaping cups). Button mushrooms don't work well in this recipe.

VEGAN, GLUTEN-FREE (use gluten-free bread if serving on buns)

per serving: calories 210 | carbs 18g | fiber 1.7g | sugar 9.3g | protein 0.4g | fat 14.8g | sodium 656mg | iron 0mg
*does not include buns

BEST BREAD

Vietnamese baguettes are best, and can often be found at local Asian supermarkets. If you can't find these, use French rolls and pop them in the air fryer to make the crust crispy (like Vietnamese bread!).

Have a question about this recipe?

Lemongrass Tofu Bánh Mì

If there's one thing that describes the dozens of bánh mì sandwiches I ate while in Southern Vietnam, it's that no bánh mì is the same. They're all different combinations of textures and flavors, precisely what this tofu version accomplishes. Zingy tofu, quick pickled veggies, spicy mayo, lots of yum.

SERVES 4 • 1 HOUR 30 MINUTES

Tofu

1 (14-ounce) block firm or extra firm tofu

2 tablespoons soy sauce

2 tablespoons rice vinegar

2 tablespoons sesame oil

1 tablespoon sugar

1 teaspoon grated ginger

1 teaspoon grated lemongrass (optional)*

Pickled Veggies

2 tablespoons rice vinegar

2 tablespoons sesame oil

½ teaspoon each salt and sugar

1 cup shredded carrots

1 cup cucumber, thinly sliced

1 jalapeno, deseeded and thinly sliced

Sauce

¼ cup mayonnaise

1 tablespoon sriracha

1 tablespoon lime juice

To Serve

4 small baguettes

½ cup cilantro, roughly chopped

Cut: Stand tofu on its side and cut down the center to create 2 to 4 thin slabs. Cut each slab in half lengthwise to create slabs that will fit into your baguettes.

Press: Press tofu for at least 15 minutes, using either a tofu press or by wrapping it in a clean towel and setting a heavy pan on top of it.

Marinate Tofu: Stir together the rest of the Tofu ingredients in a shallow dish, then add the tofu. Coat each slab, then let marinate for at least 1 hour (up to 24 hours).

Pickled Veggies: In a separate bowl, stir together all Pickled Veggies ingredients and let marinate for 1 hour.

Cook Tofu: Cook tofu over medium/high heat in a nonstick skillet, flipping to cook both sides until golden brown and crispy, about 5 minutes per side.

Assemble: Stir together Sauce ingredients and spread onto the inside of each baguette. Stuff with the tofu, pickled veggies, and cilantro.

*Fresh lemongrass can be challenging to find, but you can find a tube of lemongrass puree in the fresh herb section of most grocery stores.

VEGAN (use vegan mayo), **GLUTEN-FREE** (replace soy sauce with tamari, use gluten-free bread)

per serving: calories 580 | carbs 67.9g | fiber 4.4g | sugar 9.1g | protein 21.7g | fat 25.1g | sodium 1530mg | iron 6mg

"We LOVED this recipe! It's the closest recipe I've made that's enough like my husband's beloved Manwiches that he not only ate it but asked for seconds, and he's not the vegan in the house."

-Mary

Have a question about this recipe?

Vegan Sloppy Joes

Have you met Textured Vegetable Protein yet? She's about to be your new favorite ingredient. Otherwise known as TVP, this vegan protein is made from soy that has been dehydrated into different shapes. My favorite way to use it? As the ground beef base for vegan sloppy joes!

SERVES 6 • 30 MINUTES

2 tablespoons olive oil

1 cup diced white onion, about 1 medium onion

1 green bell pepper, diced

1 (29-ounce) can tomato sauce

1 cup vegetable broth

1 tablespoon chili powder

1 tablespoon mustard

1 tablespoon soy sauce

1 teaspoon brown sugar

1 teaspoon vegan Worcestershire sauce

Pinch each salt and pepper

1 ½ cups textured vegetable protein (TVP)

To serve: 6 hamburger buns

Flavor Base: Heat oil in a large saute pan over medium heat. Add the onion and pepper, cooking until onion is soft and translucent, about 5 minutes.

Sauce: Stir in all remaining ingredients except TVP. Bring to a gentle simmer, then add TVP.

Cook: Cover and cook for 15 minutes, stirring occasionally until mixture is thick and TVP is soft.

Serve: Spoon sloppy joe mixture onto hamburger buns and serve!

Which type?

TVP comes in many shapes and sizes. Look for the small granules for this recipe.

VEGAN

per serving: calories 250 | carbs 35.9g | fiber 5.3g | sugar 12.1g | protein 10.9g | fat 7.8g | sodium 1253mg | iron 4mg

"I'm not a vegetarian, but I like to have meatless dinners, once a week. This recipe was amazing. I felt like a chef. My husband loved it too."

-Daniela

Have a question about this recipe?

Portobello Mushroom Burgers

I used to think I didn't like mushrooms. This recipe was my gateway to liking them. Nay, loving them. Savory, meaty, grillable—it's everything a burger should be. I like to store them in the marinade until it's BBQ time (which makes them great for bringing to cookouts where you may be the only non-meat eater!).

SERVES 6 • 15 MINUTES

Portobello Mushroom Burgers

6 large portobello mushrooms

¼ cup olive oil

2 tablespoons soy sauce

2 tablespoons lemon juice

4 cloves garlic, minced

½ teaspoon each oregano, smoked paprika, salt, pepper

Fancy Sauce

2 tablespoons mayonnaise

2 tablespoons ketchup

1 clove garlic, minced

¼ teaspoon smoked paprika

To serve: burger buns, sharp cheddar cheese, sliced tomatoes, lettuce, sliced red onions

Prep Mushrooms: Clean mushrooms gently with a damp paper towel. Remove stems (and gills if you don't like the texture). In a small bowl, combine oil, soy sauce, lemon juice, garlic, and seasonings. Brush liberally onto the tops and bottoms of the mushrooms.

Cook Burgers: Heat a large non-stick skillet over medium/high. Add the mushrooms and cook for 3 minutes on each side, or until slightly softened, brushing with remaining marinade to add more flavor. Alternatively, cook on the grill for 5 minutes per side until grill lines appear. Add cheese at the last minute of cooking.

Serve: Combine all Fancy Sauce ingredients in a small bowl. Serve burgers on toasted buns with fancy sauce, tomatoes, lettuce, and onion.

What about the gills? Can you eat the gills of a Portobello mushroom? Yes! The texture can turn a little soft during cooking, so you can scrape them out if you prefer your burgers without (we like them with gills and all).

VEGAN (use vegan mayo, omit cheese), **GLUTEN-FREE** (replace soy sauce with tamari, use gluten-free buns)

per serving: calories 130 | carbs 7.2g | fiber 1.2g | sugar 2.3g | protein 3.9g | fat 10.3g | sodium 592mg | iron 1mg
(for 1 patty with fancy sauce, bun and condiments not included)

"DELICIOUS and easy. This is the "just right" mix of heat and sweet and tang. You can use frozen pre-cubed squash and eliminate the majority of time this recipe takes."

-Laurie

Have a question about this recipe?

Roasted Butternut And Chickpea Wraps

Spicy, savory flavor wrapped up in warm flatbreads is the name of the game with these wraps! Loaded with crispy roasted chickpeas and a lemony hummus sauce, this is one of my weeknight favorites. Cut the butternut in advance to save time on the day of cooking!

SERVES 4 • 40 MINUTES

Filling

½ of a butternut squash, peeled and cubed

1 (15-ounce) can chickpeas, drained and patted dry

1 medium white onion, cut into large chunks

3 tablespoons olive oil

1 tablespoon soy sauce

1 tablespoon sriracha

2 teaspoons maple syrup

1 teaspoon smoked paprika

¼ teaspoon each salt and pepper

Sauce

½ cup hummus

2 teaspoons lemon juice

2 cloves garlic, minced

Water to thin

To serve: 4 flatbreads, handful of arugula

Roast: Preheat oven to 425°F. Throw all Filling ingredients into a large bowl and toss to evenly coat. Spread onto a parchment-lined baking sheet and bake for 30 minutes, or until squash is fork-tender and chickpeas are crispy.

Sauce: Combine all Sauce ingredients, adding a touch of water to thin into a sauce consistency.

Assemble: Evenly top each flatbread with fillings, sauce, and arugula, then fold and enjoy!

Flatbreads too stiff to fold? Stack them onto each other and wrap the whole bundle in a damp paper towel. Microwave for 20 seconds, or until they're flexible enough to fold.

Great for Meal Prep!

VEGAN, GLUTEN-FREE (replace soy sauce with tamari, use gluten-free wraps)

per serving: calories 471 | carbs 57.9g | fiber 10.8g | sugar 5.7g | protein 11.8g | fat 17.3g | sodium 1004mg | iron 3.8mg

"These are legit!! They really do taste just like PF Changs lettuce wraps. Will for sure be making again!"

-Cori

Have a question about this recipe?

Copycat P.F. Chang's Lettuce Wraps

This plant-based version of chicken wraps uses a base of crumbled tofu and savory mushrooms to create a meal that doesn't miss. Pro tip: Don't skip the optional crispy rice noodles (partially because they add a fantastic texture, but mostly because they're just so fun to watch cook)!

SERVES 4 • 45 MINUTES

Lettuce Wraps

Optional: rice noodles + oil

1 (14-ounce) block firm or extra firm tofu

1 tablespoon oil (sesame oil is great here)

½ cup diced white onion, about ½ medium onion

8 ounces mushrooms, roughly chopped

2 cloves garlic, minced

1 tablespoon grated ginger

1 (8-ounce) can water chestnuts, chopped or sliced

2 tablespoons soy sauce

2 tablespoons hoisin sauce

1 tablespoon rice vinegar

½ cup sliced green onions, divided

16 butterhead lettuce leaves

Optional Sauce

This is great with a spicy mayo on top. Stir together 4 tablespoons mayo, 1 tablespoon sriracha, and a squeeze of lime.

Optional Crispy Rice Noodles: Heat about ½ inch of oil in a large saute pan over medium/high heat. Drop a single rice noodle into the oil. When it bubbles, the oil is hot enough. Working in batches, drop the noodles into the hot oil cooking for just a few seconds until they puff up. Remove from oil and set on a paper towel.

Tofu: Drain tofu and wrap in a few layers of paper towels. Squeeze to remove excess moisture, then use your hands to crumble up the tofu. Heat oil in a large saute pan or wok over medium/high, then add the tofu. Cook until it begins to brown, 7 to 10 minutes.

Veggies: Reduce heat to medium. Add the onion, mushrooms, garlic, and ginger. Cook until mushrooms have released their moisture and it evaporates. Onion should be soft at this point, about 10 minutes.

Flavor: Add water chestnuts, soy sauce, hoisin, rice vinegar, and half of the green onions. Cover and cook for 2 to 3 more minutes.

Serve: Spoon filling into each butterhead lettuce leaf, topping with remaining green onions, optional crispy rice noodles, and optional sauce.

VEGAN, GLUTEN-FREE (replace soy sauce with tamari, check label on hoisin)

per serving: calories 157 | carbs 12.7g | fiber 3.5g | sugar 5.5g | protein 11.2g | fat 7.1g | sodium 652mg | iron 4mg

Have a question about this recipe?

Chickpea Tacos With Cilantro Sauce

This recipe is for a specific type of person: one who likes chickpeas, one who likes tacos, and one who likes cilantro. If this is you, you're just 15 minutes away from a taco that may well change your life (I said what I said). The chickpeas are cooked in a pan for speed, but the air fryer and oven also work!

SERVES 4 • 15 MINUTES

Cilantro Sauce

1 cup cilantro, thick stems removed

½ cup plain yogurt

¼ cup red wine vinegar

¼ cup extra virgin olive oil

2 teaspoons Dijon mustard

2 cloves garlic

½ teaspoon each smoked paprika, cumin, black pepper

Chickpea Tacos

1 tablespoon olive oil

2 (15-ounce) cans chickpeas, drained and patted dry

1 teaspoon each salt, oregano, garlic powder, onion powder, cumin, smoked paprika

To serve: tortillas (4 large or 8 mini), diced white onion, cilantro

Sauce: Blend all Cilantro Sauce ingredients until smooth (if you have a handheld immersion blender or small blender use it here—sometimes the small ingredient amounts make this recipe tricky for larger blenders).

Cook Chickpeas: Heat oil in a large saute pan over medium/high heat. Add chickpeas and cook for about 7 minutes, until they begin to brown.

Flavor Chickpeas: Add all seasonings to the chickpeas. Stir well and continue cooking for 5 minutes, jostling the pan often, until crispy.

Assemble: Spoon chickpeas onto tortillas and top with the sauce, diced white onion, cilantro, and a squeeze of lime juice.

Oven or Air Fryer

Chickpeas can also be cooked in the air fryer (400°F for 8 to 10 minutes) or oven (400°F for 20 to 25 minutes). Stir oil and seasonings in before cooking.

VEGAN (use vegan yogurt), **GLUTEN-FREE** (use corn or gluten-free tortillas)

per serving: calories 507 | carbs 64.2g | fiber 8.5g | sugar 3.4g | protein 14.3g | fat 21.7g | sodium 1489mg | iron 4mg

Have a question about this recipe?

Bean And Cheese Tacos

I've spent many hours in hole-in-the-wall taquerias of South Texas. So, I do consider myself a connoisseur of bean and cheese tacos. Are they breakfast? Are they dinner? Are they a snack? Yes. But you know what they aren't? Vegetarian. Many refried beans contain lard, so here's my plant-based version.

SERVES 4 • 20 MINUTES

Refried Beans

2 tablespoons coconut oil

½ cup diced white onion, about ½ medium onion

4 cloves garlic, minced

1 teaspoon each cumin, oregano, smoked paprika

½ teaspoon salt

¼ teaspoon cayenne pepper

2 (15-ounce) cans pinto beans, drained and rinsed

1 cup water

1 tablespoon lime juice

Tacos

4 tortillas, flour or corn

½ cup shredded cheddar cheese

Flavor Base: Heat coconut oil in a saute pan over medium heat. Add onion and cook until soft, about 5 minutes. Add garlic, spices, and salt. Continue cooking until garlic is fragrant, about 1 minute.

Beans: Add pinto beans and water. Bring to a gentle simmer, cover, and cook for 10 minutes.

Mash: Using a potato masher or fork, roughly mash the beans. They will continue to thicken once cooled, but if they're too runny for your preference, continue cooking for a few minutes, uncovered, to thicken. Stir in lime juice.

Serve: Heat tortillas, either on the stove or in the microwave. Spread ¼ cup of beans and about 2 tablespoons of cheddar cheese into each tortilla. Fold and enjoy (or optionally cook).

Cook (optional): For a crispy exterior, cook tacos in a skillet over medium heat for 3 minutes per side, or until golden brown and crispy.

VEGAN (use a vegan cheese), **GLUTEN-FREE** (use corn or gluten-free tortillas)

per serving: calories 257 | carbs 26.7g | fiber 5.8g | sugar 1.7g | protein 9.5g | fat 12.7g | sodium 1030mg | iron 2mg

"Out of control good. I've never had tempeh until today, but I'm now a fan for life."

-Veda

Have a question about this recipe?

Kimchi Tempeh Tacos

Vegan "meat" products have come a long way, but there's just something about making it yourself—especially when it's as easy as using a box grater to turn a block of tempeh into faux ground beef. You can stop there and make it more traditionally Mexican-flavored or spice it up with kimchi and sriracha mayo!

SERVES 3 • 25 MINUTES

Taco "Meat"

1 (8-ounce) package tempeh

1 tablespoon olive oil

1 teaspoon each cumin, chili powder

½ teaspoon each salt, smoked paprika

1 clove garlic, minced

2 tablespoons tomato paste

1 tablespoon water

Taco Fillings

1 cup kimchi, chopped

1 avocado

1 handful cilantro

6 small tortillas or taco shells

Sauce

¼ cup sour cream,
can use plain Greek yogurt

¼ cup mayonnaise

1 to 2 tablespoons sriracha

1 teaspoon lime juice

Prep "Meat": Roughly grate tempeh using a box grater. Heat oil in a large saute pan over medium/high heat, then add tempeh. Cook until golden brown, about 5 minutes. Stir in remaining Taco "Meat" ingredients. Continue cooking for 5 minutes, to cook out the sourness from the tomato paste.

Prep Fillings: Optionally saute kimchi for 5 minutes to slightly caramelize it. Slice avocado and chop cilantro.

Sauce: Stir together all Sauce ingredients.

Assemble: Spoon Taco "Meat" into each tortilla, topping with kimchi, avocado, cilantro, and sauce.

VEGAN (use vegan yogurt and mayo), **GLUTEN-FREE** (use gluten-free tortillas and check tempeh packaging)

per serving: calories 674 | carbs 50.4g | fiber 7.2g | sugar 3.6g | protein 19.8g | fat 45.2g | sodium 1100mg | iron 4mg

"I just made this for the first time and oh my gosh my heart. One of the only things I miss the taste of from my meat eating days is chicken salad so I am STOKED."

-Bekka

Have a question about this recipe?

"Chicken" Salad Sandwich

It could be the sensory scientist in me, but some of my favorite recipes to develop are the ones that "trick" your brain. This chickpea salad sandwich is the most classic example, with all the usual fixings of an epic chicken salad. Make a big batch in advance for easy meals throughout the week!

SERVES 4 • 15 MINUTES

Filling

2 (15-ounce) cans chickpeas, drained

1 pink lady apple, finely diced

1 stalk celery, finely diced

¼ cup diced red onion, about ¼ medium onion

¼ cup sliced almonds

Dressing

¼ cup mayonnaise

¼ cup plain Greek yogurt

2 teaspoons Dijon mustard

1 teaspoon lemon juice

¼ teaspoon each salt and pepper

To serve: 4 croissants (cut in half but not all the way through) or 8 slices of bread

Smash: In a large bowl, roughly smash chickpeas with a fork or your fingers.

Chop: Add chopped apple, celery, and onion to the bowl of smashed chickpeas along with the almonds.

Assemble: Stir together Dressing ingredients, then add it to your chickpeas. Stir to evenly combine.

Better With Time: To really let the flavors mingle, optionally let this salad chill in the fridge for an hour before serving.

Serve: Spoon "Chicken" Salad onto bread of choice and serve!

VEGAN (use vegan mayo and yogurt), **GLUTEN-FREE** (use gluten-free bread)

per serving: calories 674 | carbs 50.4g | fiber 7.2g | sugar 3.6g | protein 19.8g | fat 45.2g | sodium 1100mg | iron 4mg
*with croissants instead of bread

"This was fantastic! My new go-to taco recipe. And I hardly ate sweet potatoes before, but will for sure be rotating them into my diet more often. So good!"

-Claudia

Have a question about this recipe?

Sweet Potato And Black Beans Tacos

Tacos are a major food group in our house. You have your dairy, your fruits, your veggies, your grains, and your tacos. This recipe puts two of our favorite ingredients—sweet potatoes and black beans—into a taco! It's drizzled with a smoky chipotle sauce that balances out the sweetness of the sweet potatoes.

SERVES 4 • 45 MINUTES

Filling

3 medium sweet potatoes

2 tablespoons olive oil

1 teaspoon each garlic powder, smoked paprika, cumin

¼ teaspoon each chili powder, salt

1 (15-ounce) can black beans, drained and rinsed

Chipotle Sauce

½ cup plain Greek yogurt

1 to 2 tablespoons adobo sauce (from a jar of chipotle peppers)*

1 tablespoon lime juice

2 cloves garlic, minced

Pinch of salt, to taste

To serve: 8 small tortillas or taco shells, cotija cheese, cilantro

Filling: Preheat oven to 425°F. Peel and dice the sweet potatoes into ½-inch cubes, then toss together with oil and spices. Spread onto a baking sheet and bake for 25 minutes. Pull out the baking sheet and add the beans, tossing to combine with the potatoes. Put back in the oven for 5 to 10 minutes, or until sweet potatoes are fork-tender and beans are hot.

Sauce: Meanwhile, stir together all Sauce ingredients, adding more or less adobo sauce to suit your spicy tolerance.

Heat Tortillas: Heat your tortillas on the stove (for soft) or in the oven (for shells).

Assembly: Spoon sweet potatoes and beans into tortillas, drizzling with sauce and desired toppings.

**Use that leftover can of chipotle peppers in adobo sauce for Enchilada Stuffed Sweet Potatoes (page 135).*

VEGAN (use vegan yogurt), **GLUTEN-FREE** (use corn gluten-free tortillas)

per serving: calories 308 | carbs 51g | fiber 8.1g | sugar 9.1g | protein 7.9g | fat 9.8g | sodium 387mg | iron 3mg

Enchilada Stuffed
Sweet Potatoes
page 135

5

Main Events

"What's for dinner?" It's a question that's pitched in houses every day all over the world. And there are over 500 recipes on Live Eat Learn that aim to answer this question, but these are the very best.

These are the recipes that feed everyone, from the protein-hungry carnivores to the vegetarians to the vegans to the somewhere-in-betweenians. The recipes that I've cooked for years in my kitchen, and that our readers rave about. These are the main events!

In this chapter:

Have a question about this recipe?

Chickpea Meatballs

I'll just come out and say it: we are not a pasta household. You likely won't catch me eating a bowl of spaghetti for dinner. But where I compromise is meatballs. A good meatball is the only way I'll do spaghetti, and this easy recipe is my go-to. (But don't limit yourself to pasta; they're great on sandwiches or by themselves!)

SERVES 6 • 1 HOUR

2 (15-ounce) cans chickpeas, drained and patted dry

1 cup breadcrumbs

3 large eggs

½ cup Italian (flat-leaf) parsley, thick stems removed

4 cloves garlic

½ of a medium red onion, roughly chopped

2 teaspoons each Italian seasoning, smoked paprika, black pepper

1 teaspoon salt

For cooking: oil

Blend: Add all ingredients (except oil) to a food processor. Pulse, scraping down the sides as needed, until evenly combined (it's okay if there's still some texture to it, blend until it's more or less mixed into a dough). If dough is very soft or sticky, add a tablespoon of flour.

Roll: Form 25 to 30 chickpea meatballs. To ensure the meatballs stay super round when cooking, set them on a parchment-lined plate and freeze them for 15 minutes before cooking.

Cook: Generously coat the bottom of a large saute pan in oil over medium heat. Add meatballs, ensuring they remain in a single layer. Cook, flipping them often, until meatballs are browned on all sides and firm when poked. Cooking should take 15 to 20 minutes.

Serve warm in your favorite meatball dishes, like with spaghetti or on a meatball sub!

Make it vegan!

Make these vegan by using flax eggs. Stir together 3 tablespoons of ground flaxseed with 8 tablespoons of water, then use that in place of the eggs.

VEGAN (see notes), **GLUTEN-FREE** (use gluten-free breadcrumbs)

per serving: calories 249 | carbs 42.1g | fiber 6.5g | sugar 1.7g | protein 11.5g | fat 9.2g | sodium 912mg | iron 3mg

"I made this last night! They were so good! They were our main course!"

-Melinda

Have a question about this recipe?

Herby Ricotta Stuffed Peppers

These stuffed peppers taste straight out of Tuscany, with fresh herbs, creamy ricotta, and sharp parmesan. Ready in about an hour (with minimal hands-on time), they're a simple dish packed with flavor. My favorite part of this recipe? The fennel seed! As a spice drawer minimalist, I would still recommend getting this if you don't yet have it.

SERVES 4 • 1 HOUR

Peppers

4 bell peppers, any color

1 tablespoon olive oil

Filling

4 cups spinach

1 (15-ounce) tub ricotta cheese

1 cup shredded mozzarella cheese

½ cup grated parmesan cheese

2 large eggs

4 green onions, sliced

½ cup basil, chopped

½ cup Italian (flat-leaf) parsley, thick stems removed then chopped

1 teaspoon each dried rosemary, dried thyme, salt, fennel seed (roughly chop the fennel seeds to release their flavor)

½ teaspoon black pepper

Topping

½ cup breadcrumbs

1 tablespoon olive oil

Prep: Preheat oven to 400°F. Cut bell peppers in half lengthwise, removing seeds and ribs. Set peppers cut side up on a parchment-lined baking sheet and brush all over with olive oil. Bake for about 20 minutes, or until they begin to soften. When finished, drain the water out of each pepper and reduce oven temperature to 350°F.

Mix: Meanwhile, in a microwave-safe bowl, microwave spinach for 15 to 30 seconds, or until wilted down. Roughly chop, then combine it with all remaining Filling ingredients.

Stuff: Stuff peppers evenly with the filling.

Topping: In a small bowl, combine breadcrumbs and oil. Sprinkle evenly over the peppers, pressing it into the filling so it sticks.

Bake: Return peppers to oven and bake for 30 minutes. If the tops aren't golden brown at this point, turn on the broiler and let them brown, watching closely until they're done (it won't take more than a minute or two).

You can use a variety of pepper colors for a fun presentation or go with all one color. Red peppers are sweeter, while green peppers are slightly more bitter.

GLUTEN-FREE (use gluten-free breadcrumbs)

per serving: calories 386 | carbs 22.3g | fiber 3.5g | sugar 3.5g | protein 24.5g | fat 22.8g | sodium 1047mg | iron 4mg

Have a question about this recipe?

Hidden Veggie Pasta Sauce

When the name of the game is "clean out all the sad, soon-to-go bad vegetables in the kitchen," roast and blend them into a creamy pasta sauce. While I've included my go-to veggies in this recipe, most will work here. (Just keep in mind what color they might blend into if you're trying to keep these veggies a secret.)

SERVES 6 • 1 HOUR

- 4 tomatoes, any variety
- 8 ounces mushrooms
- 1 red bell pepper
- 1 medium red onion
- 1 zucchini
- 4 tablespoons olive oil, divided
- 2 teaspoons Italian seasoning
- 1 bulb of garlic
- 8 ounces feta cheese
- ½ cup heavy cream
- To serve: your pasta of choice

Prep Veggies: Preheat oven to 400°F. Chop all veggies into chunks. Throw them onto a large baking sheet, drizzle with 3 tablespoons of the oil, and sprinkle with seasoning, tossing to coat evenly.

Prep Garlic: Trim the top off the bulb of garlic to expose the top of each clove. Pour 1 tablespoon of the oil over garlic so that it seeps into the cloves, then wrap the whole bulb in aluminum foil. Place it on the tray with the veggies.

Roast: Transfer baking sheet to the oven and cook for 30 to 40 minutes, or until veggies are tender and a bit charred. Garlic should be soft and golden brown.

Pasta: When veggies are almost finished cooking, prepare your choice of pasta. When finished, reserve ½ cup of the pasta water before draining.

Blend: Transfer roasted veggies to a blender. Squeeze the roasted garlic cloves out and add them (you can add as many or few as you want). Add feta, cream, and ¼ cup of the pasta water. Blend until smooth, adding more pasta water as needed to reach your desired consistency. Mix into pasta and serve warm.

Other veggies that work well in this recipe: cauliflower, sweet potato, eggplant, green cabbage, parsnip, butternut squash, pumpkin, carrot, broccoli, radish

---

GLUTEN-FREE

per serving: calories 249 | carbs 12g | fiber 2.1g | sugar 7.3g | protein 7.7g | fat 19.7g | sodium 437mg | iron 1mg
*does not include pasta

"My biggest complaint about this recipe is that I've now eaten 2 pounds of pasta over the past 2 weeks, ha! It's so addicting! I make it on Sunday and then pack it for lunch for the rest of the week."

-Kellie

Have a question about this recipe?

Miso Pasta

The rich, savory flavors of miso paste combined with cracked black pepper and freshly grated Parmesan cheese. It's like a next-level cacio e pepe. You can use any type of pasta here, but I prefer a thick, slurpy shape like bucatini.

SERVES 4 to 6 • 20 MINUTES

1 pound bucatini pasta

¼ cup unsalted butter

¼ cup white miso paste

1 teaspoon coarsely ground black pepper

1 cup grated parmesan cheese

Cook Pasta: Bring a large pot of heavily salted water to a boil. Cook bucatini according to instructions on package. When finished, reserve 1 cup of the pasta water and drain the rest.

Make Sauce: Meanwhile, in a large saute pan over medium heat combine butter, miso, and pepper. Cook until butter is melted and pepper is fragrant, about 2 minutes.

Assemble: After draining pasta and dumping it back into the large pot, add 1 cup of the reserved pasta water back into the pot of pasta, along with miso butter sauce and parmesan. Stir vigorously for 2 minutes until cheese is melted and noodles are coated with sauce. Serve immediately!

GLUTEN-FREE (use gluten-free pasta)

per serving: calories 536 | carbs 70g | fiber 3g | sugar 6g | protein 22.5g | fat 18.7g | sodium 890mg | iron 3mg

Have a question
about this recipe?

Marry Me Pesto Pasta

This pasta is based on the same concept as Marry Me Chicken—so good it could lead to a marriage proposal from the person you serve it to. The secret? A creamy Tuscan sauce with flavors of sun-dried tomatoes, butter, garlic, and cream. I'll sometimes throw in a plant-based spicy ground sausage to seal the deal.

SERVES 4 • 15 MINUTES

8 ounces pasta, any type (pappardelle pictured)

2 tablespoons unsalted butter

4 cloves garlic, minced

½ teaspoon each salt, oregano, red pepper flakes

¼ teaspoon ground black pepper

½ cup sun-dried tomatoes, roughly chopped

½ cup pesto

½ cup heavy cream

½ cup grated parmesan cheese

Pasta: Cook pasta according to package instructions. Reserve ¼ cup of the pasta water before draining the pasta.

Flavor Base: Heat butter, garlic, salt, oregano, red pepper flakes, and black pepper in a large saute pan or pot over medium heat. Cook for about 2 minutes, until garlic is fragrant.

Make It Sauce: Reduce heat to medium/low. Stir in reserved pasta water, sun-dried tomatoes, pesto, and cream. Let cook for a few minutes, just to heat the sauce.

Finish: Remove from heat then stir in parmesan and cooked pasta. Serve warm.

DIY PESTO

To make your own pesto, pulse together in a food processor:

2 ½ cups fresh basil

¼ cup pine nuts

½ cup grated parmesan

4 cloves garlic

½ teaspoon each salt and pepper

½ cup extra virgin olive oil

GLUTEN-FREE (use gluten-free pasta)

per serving: calories 475 | carbs 48.6g | fiber 2.8g | sugar 2.1g | protein 13.8g | fat 25.8g | sodium 260mg | iron 2mg

Have a question about this recipe?

Spaghetti Squash Alfredo Casserole

I love a low-ingredient recipe, and this one always fits the bill. But I also love a recipe that can be adapted, which is where this casserole shines. You can add more broccoli (or a different veggie altogether), stir in some pesto, or stuff the mixture back into the squash shells for serving. Have fun making this recipe your own!

SERVES 4 • 45 MINUTES

2 medium spaghetti squash

2 cups broccoli florets

2 tablespoons olive oil

1 (16-ounce) jar Alfredo sauce, about 1 ½ cups

1 cup shredded mozzarella cheese, divided

Generous pinch of ground black pepper

Prep: Preheat oven to 400°F. Cut spaghetti squash in half and scoop out the seeds. Drizzle the insides with half of the oil and rub to evenly coat. Place cut-side down on a baking sheet and prick the outside with a fork. Spread broccoli florets onto the same baking sheet and drizzle with remaining oil, tossing to coat.

Roast: Roast for about 30 minutes, or until squash is fork tender. Broccoli should be lightly browned. (If it cooks too quickly, take it out of the oven earlier than the squash.) When squash is finished, flip it over and allow to cool enough to touch.

Spaghettify: Use a fork to scrape strands from the inside of the spaghetti squash.

Assemble: In a large bowl stir together spaghetti squash strands, roasted broccoli, Alfredo sauce, and ½ cup of the cheese. Pour into a large casserole dish (or back into the spaghetti squash shell) and gently pack into an even layer. Sprinkle with remaining ½ cup of cheese.

Broil: Turn your oven to "broil" (about 550°F) and add casserole dish. Cook for just a few minutes, watching closely until the cheese has melted and turned golden brown. Top generously with freshly ground black pepper.

Veggie Power

Feel free to pack even more roasted veggies into this recipe. Cauliflower, zucchini, and eggplant all work well.

GLUTEN-FREE

per serving: calories 318 | carbs 20.2g | fiber 1.2g | sugar 2.8g | protein 9.6g | fat 24.6g | sodium 792mg | iron 1mg

Veggie Lasagna With Béchamel

My vegetable lasagna consists of a handful of main ingredients. It's your typical lasagna—noodles, marinara, cheese, and veggies—but with an authentic twist. Instead of ricotta, which I find makes lasagna dry and gritty, we're using a rich and velvety béchamel. (To make ahead, use same instructions as Baked Ziti, page 114.)

SERVES 6 to 8 • 1 HOUR 30 MINUTES

Lasagna Veggies

1 tablespoon olive oil

1 eggplant, peeled or unpeeled and diced

1 zucchini, peeled or unpeeled and diced

1 red bell pepper, diced

1 handful spinach, roughly chopped

2 cloves garlic, minced

Béchamel Sauce

2 cups milk

4 tablespoons unsalted butter

¼ cup all-purpose flour

½ cup grated parmesan cheese

¼ teaspoon each salt and pepper

Remaining Ingredients

1 (24-ounce) jar marinara sauce (or make it homemade, page 39)

1 (12-ounce) box no-boil lasagna noodles

2 cups shredded mozzarella cheese

"This has become our go-to recipe for lasagna. It is flavorful, delicious, and so easy to prep work wise. It's so yummy and every friend we've had over who has tried this has agreed with us."

-Kathy

Veggies: Heat oil in a large saute pan over medium heat. Add eggplant, zucchini, and bell pepper, cooking until veggies are soft, about 10 minutes. Add spinach and garlic and cook, stirring constantly until wilted down, about 1 minute.

Béchamel: Heat milk in the microwave until warm. Melt butter in a medium pot over medium heat. Whisk in the flour, cooking and stirring until the mixture no longer smells like raw flour, about 2 minutes. Slowly whisk in the milk, stirring well to evenly combine. Bring the mixture to a simmer and cook until thickened, about 5 minutes. Remove from heat then stir in parmesan, salt, and pepper.

Assemble: Preheat oven to 350°F then layer:

Bottom – Spread ½ cup of marinara onto the bottom of a large casserole dish (9×13 inch or similar). Layer in one third of the lasagna noodles.

First Layer – one third of the béchamel, half of the veggies, one third of the mozzarella, and 1 cup of marinara. Top with one third of the lasagna noodles.

Second Layer – one third of the béchamel, remaining veggies, one third of the mozzarella, and 1 cup of marinara. Top with remaining lasagna noodles.

Top – Spoon on remaining béchamel, remaining marinara, and sprinkle on remaining mozzarella.

Bake: Cover tightly with aluminum foil and bake for 45 minutes, or until bubbling at the edges. Remove foil, increase temperature to 400°F, and continue cooking until the top is golden brown, 8 to 10 minutes.

Rest: Allow lasagna to sit uncovered on the counter for 15 to 30 minutes before serving to help layers firm up.

per serving: calories 441 | carbs 59g | fiber 6.6g | sugar 12g | protein 15g | fat 16.8g | sodium 557mg | iron 3mg (assuming 6 servings)

MAKE AHEAD

Assemble everything into your baking dish, then tightly wrap in plastic wrap and store in the fridge until ready to bake (up to 3 days). Can also be frozen to be baked later. Freeze the assembled ziti for up to a month. When ready to cook, allow the ziti to thaw in the refrigerator, then bake as directed.

Have a question about this recipe?

Vegetable Baked Ziti

Baked ziti is like a laid-back lasagna, with many of the same flavors (without the perfect layering or béchamel). It's the kind of dinner you can throw in a bowl and cozy up with on the couch. Or make ahead for busy weeks. Or impress your dinner guests with (it feeds six hungry adults). Baked ziti is whatever you need it to be.

SERVES 6 to 8 • 1 HOUR

Pasta

1 pound uncooked ziti pasta, can also use penne or rigatoni

Veggie Sauce

2 tablespoons olive oil

1 zucchini, peeled or unpeeled and diced

1 eggplant, peeled or unpeeled and diced

1 red bell pepper, diced

1 cup diced white onion, about 1 medium onion

3 cloves garlic, minced

2 (24-ounce) jars marinara sauce (or make it homemade, page 39)

¼ cup basil, chopped

1 teaspoon oregano

¼ teaspoon salt

Ricotta Mixture

1 (15-ounce) tub ricotta cheese

10 ounces frozen spinach, thawed and squeezed dry(ish)

¼ cup grated parmesan cheese

Cheese

1 cup shredded mozzarella cheese

¼ cup grated parmesan cheese

Pasta: Bring a large pot of water to a boil then add a generous dash of salt (it should taste like ocean water). Add pasta and cook according to the instructions on the package, until al dente. When finished, drain and cover.

Veggie Sauce: Add oil to a large saute pan or pot over medium heat. Add zucchini, eggplant, pepper, onion, and garlic, cooking until they're slightly softened, 5 to 7 minutes. Stir in marinara, basil, oregano, and salt, cover, and let gently simmer for 15 minutes.

Ricotta Mixture: In a bowl, stir together ricotta cheese, thawed spinach, and parmesan.

Cheese: In a separate bowl, mix together mozzarella and parmesan.

Assemble: Preheat oven to 350°F. In a large casserole dish (9×13 inch or similar) layer:

half of the veggie sauce, half of the pasta, half of the ricotta mixture, half of the cheese

then repeat that with:

remaining veggie sauce, remaining pasta, remaining ricotta mixture, remaining cheese.

Bake for about 30 minutes, or until cheese is golden and melted, and sauce is bubbling around the edges. If the cheese browns too quickly, cover the dish with aluminum foil. Allow it to rest for a few minutes before serving.

GLUTEN-FREE (use gluten-free pasta)

per serving: calories 475 | carbs 62.9g | fiber 8.3g | sugar 11.8g | protein 8.3g | fat 15.6g | sodium 605mg | iron 4mg (assuming 6 servings)

Risotto

I'm what you might call...obsessed with risotto. It's rich, creamy, and incredibly customizable. Over the years, I've created many risotto recipes, which typically all have the same base. Use the classic recipe below or customize it with a flavor!

SERVES 4 • 45 MINUTES

Classic Risotto

4 to 6 cups vegetable broth

1 tablespoon unsalted butter

½ cup finely diced shallots, about 2 medium shallots

2 cloves garlic, minced

1 teaspoon salt

1 ½ cups arborio rice

1 cup dry white wine, optional (if not using wine, use 1 extra cup of broth)

1 cup grated parmesan cheese

2 tablespoons heavy cream

To serve: ground black pepper

Broth: Pour broth into a pot and set it over low heat on the stove to stay warm.

Flavor Base: Melt butter in a high-sided saute pan over medium heat. Add shallots and garlic, cooking until shallots are soft, about 3 minutes.

Toast Rice: Add salt and rice then cook, stirring frequently for about 2 minutes, until the rice is opaque on the outside but uncooked on the inside.

Add Wine (Optional): Add wine to the pan and simmer until wine has completely been absorbed.

Cook Rice: Slowly add the vegetable broth while stirring rice often, adding ½ cup at a time. Wait until broth is completely absorbed before adding another ½ cup, continuing this process until rice is cooked fully. Begin tasting the rice after 20 minutes. Once it is cooked through, stop adding broth (you may not need it all).

Serve: Stir in parmesan cheese and cream. Serve warm, topped with freshly ground black pepper.

per serving: calories 340 | carbs 41.4g | fiber 1.3g | sugar 1g | protein 14.2g | fat 9.5g | sodium 1357mg | iron 1mg

GLUTEN-FREE

Have a question about this recipe?

Mushroom Risotto

Classic risotto ingredients plus:

1 lb mushrooms,
like button, shiitake, portobello, or wild mushrooms

1 tablespoon unsalted butter

Before making risotto as directed, cook mushrooms. Clean then slice the mushrooms. Heat 1 tablespoon of the butter over medium heat in a large saute pan. Add mushrooms and cook until they release their moisture then brown slightly, about 10 minutes. Remove mushrooms from the pan.

Cook risotto as instructed, then stir cooked mushrooms into the risotto before serving.

Pepper Gorgonzola Risotto

Classic risotto ingredients plus:

4 green onions, sliced

1 red bell pepper, chopped

2 handfuls spinach, chopped

Reduce parmesan to ¼ cup

¼ cup crumbled gorgonzola

Make risotto as directed, but at the final step, stir in green onions, bell pepper, spinach, parmesan, and gorgonzola. Finish with a squeeze of fresh lemon juice and ground black pepper.

Saffron Risotto (Risotto Alla Milanese)

Classic risotto ingredients plus:

½ teaspoon saffron threads

Make risotto as directed, but add saffron to the warming broth in the 1st step.

Lemon Basil Risotto

Classic risotto ingredients plus:

3 stalks celery, finely chopped

Zest and juice from ½ of a lemon

2 tablespoons fresh basil

Make risotto as directed, adding celery to the pan at the same time as the shallots. Continue following the directions until the end, where you'll stir in the lemon zest, juice, and basil before serving.

Truffle Risotto

Classic risotto ingredients plus:

2 tablespoons truffle oil

Optional: fresh truffle

Make risotto as directed, stirring truffle oil in at the final step. Feeling extra fancy? Thinly shave fresh truffle onto each plate of risotto before serving (I find these on Etsy).

Goat Cheese And Leek Risotto

Classic risotto ingredients plus:

Omit shallots

2 medium leeks, finely sliced

½ cup frozen peas

Reduce parmesan to ½ cup

2 tablespoons soft goat cheese

Make risotto as directed, but replace the shallots with leeks. At the end of cooking, stir in frozen peas, parmesan, and goat cheese. Finish with a squeeze of fresh lemon juice and freshly ground black pepper.

Photos on next page →

Mushroom Risotto

Pepper Gorgonzola Risotto

Saffron Risotto

Lemon Basil Risotto

Truffle Risotto

Goat Cheese & Leek Risotto

main events

Butternut Squash Risotto

SERVES 4 • 1 HOUR

Classic risotto ingredients plus:

3 cups diced butternut squash, about ½ of a medium squash

Flavor Base: Heat the butter over medium heat. Stir in diced butternut squash, the shallots, and garlic. Cover with a lid and cook until the butternut is slightly soft, about 10 to 15 minutes. Roughly mash so that about half of the squash is smashed. Transfer butternut mixture out of the pan.

Toast Rice: Add salt and rice then cook, stirring frequently for about 2 minutes, until the rice is opaque on the outside but uncooked on the inside.

Resume Classic Risotto Recipe: From here, add the butternut squash mash back into the pan with the rice and resume cooking as directed (starting at Step 3 - Add Wine). The butternut will cook with the risotto into a vibrant, flavorful dish!

"I couldn't believe there wasn't ground meat in it. I am not a vegetarian, but this is a recipe I will definitely be making again and again. Froze some for my daughter, who is vegetarian, and she LOVED it."

-Christa

Have a question about this recipe?

Tofu Bolognese

This bolognese does things a bit differently. Aside from the obvious (no meat), we're baking the seasoned tofu into flavorful crumbles before mixing it with tomato sauce. With just a handful of pantry staple ingredients, it's a quick recipe that rivals any spaghetti with meat sauce.

SERVES 4 • 50 MINUTES

1 (14-ounce) block firm or extra firm tofu

2 tablespoons nutritional yeast

2 tablespoons soy sauce

1 tablespoon olive oil

1 teaspoon smoked paprika

½ teaspoon each garlic powder, onion powder, chili powder

1 (24-ounce) jar tomato sauce

½ pound uncooked pasta, like tagliatelle or pappardelle

Prep: Preheat oven to 350°F. Drain and dry the tofu, then crumble it into small pieces.

Flavor: Stir together crumbled tofu, nutritional yeast, soy sauce, oil, and spices.

Bake: Spread tofu in a single layer onto a parchment-lined baking sheet. Bake for 30 to 45 minutes, or until tofu is browned and a bit crispy at the edges.

Bolognese: Heat tomato sauce (on the stove or in the microwave), then stir in cooked tofu.

Pasta: Cook pasta according to instructions on package.

Assemble: Stir together pasta and sauce and serve hot!

Sauce Ratio

I like more sauce on my pasta (see "Not Really A Pasta Person" page 101), but if you prefer less, increase pasta to one pound.

VEGAN, GLUTEN-FREE (replace soy sauce with tamari)

per serving: calories 306 | carbs 39.7g | fiber 2.7g | sugar 1.9g | protein 16.9g | fat 9.7g | sodium 786mg | iron 8mg

"I made this dish for the first time about a month ago and last week my boyfriend proposed. Could be a coincidence, but also could be the power of delicious Tuscan cooking."

-Kyra

Have a question about this recipe?

Marry Me Chickpeas

Marry Me Chicken has had its moment; now it's time for Marry Me Chickpeas. This is a creamy, Tuscan-inspired dish that doesn't skimp on flavor. Serve it over rice, veggies, pasta, or simply sop it up with some good crusty bread. (If that doesn't convince you, this is the #1 most popular recipe on Live Eat Learn!)

SERVES 4 • 15 MINUTES

2 tablespoons unsalted butter

4 cloves garlic, minced

½ teaspoon each salt, oregano, red pepper flakes

¼ teaspoon ground black pepper

½ cup sun-dried tomatoes, roughly chopped

1 cup vegetable broth

2 (15-ounce) cans chickpeas, drained

1 cup heavy cream, can use half-and-half

½ cup grated parmesan cheese

2 tablespoons fresh basil, chopped

Flavor Base: Heat butter, garlic, and seasonings in a large saute pan or pot over medium heat. Cook for about 2 minutes, until garlic is fragrant.

Fillings: Stir in sun-dried tomatoes, broth, and chickpeas. Continue cooking on medium, uncovered, for 5 minutes. If you'd like it thicker, continue cooking uncovered for 5 to 10 more minutes.

Finish: Remove from heat. Stir in cream, parmesan, and basil. Serve warm with crusty bread, over rice, with pasta, or with veggies!

Change it up! Instead of the chickpeas, you can use gnocchi (add 1 extra cup of broth and add gnocchi after the 2nd step, cooking for about 3 minutes), mushrooms (saute before adding), or butter beans (straight from the can). You can also load in veggies like spinach, kale, zucchini, cauliflower, or broccoli (cook before adding), or a cooked vegan sausage.

Gnocchi with vegan spicy sausage and spinach

Button mushrooms

Butter beans with spinach

VEGAN (use coconut milk and vegan parmesan), **GLUTEN-FREE**

per serving: calories 432 | carbs 44.2g | fiber 8.3g | sugar 0.8g | protein 15.7g | fat 22.3g | sodium 1204mg | iron 3mg

"This is DELICIOUS! I was a bit skeptical about the dressing mainly...it is sooo good! You were absolutely right about the depth of flavor which was quite shocking considering it is missing anchovies (which I happen to love)."

-Jean

Have a question about this recipe?

Creamy Caesar Beans

For another recipe to inspire that can of beans in your pantry, I bring you creamy, zingy Caesar Beans. To make this Caesar dressing vegetarian, we're omitting the anchovies and adding that same depth of flavor with Dijon, mayo, and parmesan. The parmesan brings major umami, so buy a good wedge and grate it yourself.

SERVES 4 • 15 MINUTES

2 tablespoons extra virgin olive oil

2 tablespoons mayonnaise

2 tablespoons Dijon mustard

1 tablespoon lemon juice

2 cloves garlic, minced

1 (15-ounce) can white beans, like Cannelli or Great Northern

½ cup grated parmesan cheese

¼ teaspoon ground black pepper

To serve: 4 slices sourdough

Caesar: Add oil, mayo, mustard, lemon juice, and garlic to a blender. Blitz just until combined. Do not over-blend, as this can cause the sauce to break.

(If you have a handheld immersion blender or small blender use it here—sometimes the small ingredient amounts make this recipe tricky for larger blenders.)

Beans: Drain and rinse beans. Combine them with the Caesar dressing, parmesan, and black pepper.

Serve: Toast slices of sourdough and spoon Caesar beans on top. Serve immediately.

Optional Broil: To level it up, place the prepared toast under the oven broiler very briefly to toast the top and make the cheese melty!

GLUTEN-FREE (serve on gluten-free bread)

per serving: calories 326 | carbs 44.1g | fiber 5g | sugar 2g | protein 12g | fat 12g | sodium 639mg | iron 3mg

Have a question about this recipe?

Roasted Vegetable Sorghum Bowls

In food science, there's a principle called "Sensory Specific Satiety," which basically says that food becomes less pleasant when it has a lot of the same flavors and textures. Fortunately, there's no chance of that happening with this recipe. Bursting with different colors, flavors, and textures, everyone will be finishing their plates!

SERVES 2 • 1 HOUR

Sorghum

1 cup uncooked sorghum

3 cups water

Roasted Vegetables

2 medium carrots

½ pound Brussels sprouts (about 2 cups)

1 medium red onion

1 lemon

1 big bunch of thyme, about 20 sprigs, divided

2 tablespoons olive oil

Pinch of salt and pepper

Everything Else

3 tablespoons olive oil

½ cup crumbled feta cheese, divided

Pinch of salt and pepper

¼ cup dried cherries

¼ cup sliced almonds

Sorghum: Combine sorghum and water in a large pot. Bring to a boil, then reduce to a simmer. Cover and cook for 45 to 60 minutes, until water is absorbed and sorghum is tender, then fluff it with a fork.

Prep Veggies: Preheat oven to 450°F. Peel and cut carrots into ¼-inch coins. Trim and halve or quarter the Brussels sprouts. Peel and cut onion into large chunks. Zest the lemon (reserve zest for later), then cut the lemon in half.

Roast Veggies: Place veggies, lemon, and half of the thyme sprigs onto a baking sheet and drizzle with oil, salt, and pepper. Toss to coat everything. Bake for 25 minutes, or until veggies are soft and brown at the edges. Discard thyme sprigs.

Dressing: Squeeze the lemon juice from the roasted lemons into a bowl. Stir in 3 tablespoons of olive oil, half of the feta, and season with salt and pepper. Stir about a third of the dressing into the cooked sorghum.

Assemble: In a large bowl, toss together roasted vegetables, reserved lemon zest, remaining thyme leaves, remaining feta, remaining dressing, cherries, and almonds. Spoon cooked sorghum into serving bowls, topping with roasted vegetable mixture.

Ancient Grains

Sorghum is truly an ancient grain, dating back to 8000 B.C.E.! If you can't find it, feel free to substitute it with another grain, like quinoa, wild rice, freekeh, or farro.

VEGAN (omit feta), **GLUTEN-FREE**

per serving: calories 704 | carbs 57g | fiber 13g | sugar 19.3g | protein 15.3g | fat 50g | sodium 569mg | iron 3mg

Veggie Boost

Sneak in some veggies, like shredded carrots and zucchini or minced cauliflower and broccoli!

Have a question about this recipe?

Impossibly Good "Meatloaf"

Vegetarian meatloaf has never been so easy (or so delicious)! You'll love this plant-based twist on an old favorite with ingredients like mushrooms, plant-based ground beef, and the ketchup topping. It all blends together in the food processor before being baked into that classic loaf.

SERVES 6 • 1 HOUR 15 MINUTES

Meatloaf

1 pound mushrooms, button or baby bella

½ of a medium white onion, cut into chunks

3 cloves garlic

1 (12-ounce) package plant-based ground beef

1 cup breadcrumbs

1 tablespoon Italian seasoning

1 tablespoon vegan Worcestershire sauce

½ teaspoon salt

2 large eggs

Ketchup Topping

½ cup ketchup

1 tablespoon brown sugar

1 tablespoon mustard

Blitz: Preheat oven to 350°F. Add mushrooms, onion, and garlic to a food processor. Blitz until roughly broken down. (You may need to work in batches, depending on the size of your food processor.)

Mix: Stir together mushroom mixture and all remaining Meatloaf ingredients.

Topping: In a separate bowl, stir together all Ketchup Topping ingredients.

Assemble: Line a loaf pan (9×5 inch or similar) with parchment paper. Spoon meatloaf mixture into the pan, pressing to fill any gaps or empty corners. Spoon half of the Ketchup Topping onto the meatloaf, spreading it evenly over the whole top.

Bake: Bake, uncovered, for 30 minutes. Remove from oven, spread the remaining Ketchup Topping over the meatloaf, then bake for another 30 minutes. Let cool slightly before cutting into slices and serving.

"This is the absolute best vegan (I substituted flax eggs for eggs) meatloaf recipe I have ever had. Made it for my dad and male best friend who are both very much not vegan and they both loved it." -Devon

VEGAN (use 2 flax eggs: 2 tablespoons flaxseed meal mixed with 5 tablespoons water), **GLUTEN-FREE** (use gluten-free breadcrumbs)

per serving: calories 271 | carbs 29g | fiber 4.5g | sugar 9.6g | protein 17g | fat 10.3g | sodium 787mg | iron 6mg

"I generally make a double batch so we can freeze half of it and pull it out when we need a quick dinner. We think it freezes really well. Amazing!!"

-Jessica

Have a question about this recipe?

Tikka Masala Inspired Chickpeas

I can't really call this recipe "Chickpea Tikka Masala" because to truly be "tikka" style, the chickpeas would have to be marinated for hours and then grilled. And we just can't fit all that in 20 minutes! This recipe is inspired by the flavors of the classic Indian dish but is ready in a fraction of the time.

SERVES 4 • 20 MINUTES

1 tablespoon olive oil

1 cup diced white onion, about 1 medium onion

4 cloves garlic, minced

2 tablespoons grated ginger

1 tablespoon garam masala

2 teaspoons each cumin, ground coriander, turmeric, smoked paprika

1 teaspoon salt

2 (15-ounce) cans chickpeas, drained

1 (28-ounce) can tomato puree

1 (13-ounce) can full-fat coconut milk

To serve: basmati rice, naan, cilantro

Rice: If serving with rice, start cooking rice now and cover to keep warm when finished.

Saute: Heat oil in a large pot over medium heat. Add onion, cooking until soft and translucent, about 5 minutes. Add garlic and ginger and continue cooking for 1 minute, until fragrant. Stir in seasonings to coat everything evenly.

Combine: Add chickpeas, tomato puree, and coconut milk. Cover and cook, stirring occasionally, until hot and simmering, as little as 10 minutes and up to 45 minutes.

Serve: Serve hot over a mound of rice with naan and cilantro.

CHANGE IT UP

I love the simplicity of chickpeas here, but this recipe also works well with sauteed cubed eggplant or crispy sauteed tofu! Toss each with a generous spoonful of garam masala before cooking, then add to the curry at the same time as you would add the chickpeas.

Great for Meal Prep

Make a batch and portion into containers for the week, storing chickpeas separately from the rice and naan until ready to enjoy.

VEGAN, GLUTEN-FREE (use gluten-free naan)

per serving: calories 526 | carbs 70g | fiber 14.7g | sugar 14g | protein 15g | fat 24.3g | sodium 1198mg | iron 8.6mg

*without rice or naan

"I LOVED this recipe!!! Seriously so easy and delicious. I made it in a meal prep with brown rice and steamed green beans, but next time I think I'll try it on a salad to add some protein!"

-Alex

Have a question about this recipe?

Crispy Lemon Pepper Tofu

It was only recently that I discovered the joy of lemon pepper seasoning. As a proud spice drawer minimalist, I'm always skeptical of spice blends, which take up valuable real estate in my small kitchen. But for lemon pepper seasoning, I make exceptions. This simple dish celebrates that sunshiney lemon pepper flavor.

SERVES 4 • 30 MINUTES

1 (14-ounce) block firm or extra firm tofu, drained

1 tablespoon cornstarch

1 tablespoon lemon pepper seasoning

½ teaspoon salt

To serve: rice, veggies

Prep: Preheat oven to 425°F. Pat tofu dry with a clean towel, then break it into bite-sized chunks. In a large bowl, stir together cornstarch, lemon pepper seasoning, and salt. Add tofu and toss to evenly coat.

To Bake: Arrange tofu pieces on a greased baking sheet and bake for about 25 minutes, flipping halfway through cooking, until golden brown and crispy.

or

To Air Fry: Preheat your air fryer to 375°F. Add tofu to your air fryer basket or tray in a single layer. Cook for 10 to 15 minutes, shaking the pan occasionally to promote even cooking.

Serve: Serve warm with rice and/or a veggie, like broccoli or asparagus!

DIY LEMON PEPPER SEASONING

Set your oven to its lowest temperature and spread ½ cup grated lemon zest on a parchment-lined baking sheet. Put the zest in the oven until it's completely dry, anywhere from 30 minutes to an hour. Once the zest is completely dried, mix it with 2 tablespoons black pepper, 1 tablespoon flaky sea salt, 1 teaspoon onion powder, and 1 teaspoon garlic powder. For a more even consistency, you can blitz the mixture in a spice grinder.

1

2

3

VEGAN, GLUTEN-FREE

per serving: calories 104 | carbs 4g | fiber 0.5g | sugar 0.6g | protein 11.3g | fat 6.6g | sodium 340mg | iron 2mg

Enchilada Stuffed Sweet Potatoes

It's probably against some cardinal plant-based rule not to like sweet potatoes, but I find them too sweet and mushy in their plain form. This recipe changes that, balancing the sweet mush with savory, spicy flavors and a variety of textures that even sweet potato critics can get on board with.

SERVES 4 • 1 HOUR 15 MINUTES

Stuffed Sweet Potatoes

4 medium sweet potatoes

1 tablespoon olive oil

1 cup diced red onion, about 1 medium onion

1 red bell pepper, diced

2 cloves garlic, minced

1 (15-ounce) can corn, drained

1 (15-ounce) can black beans, drained and rinsed

¼ cup sour cream

2 to 4 adobo peppers in chipotle sauce, minced

½ teaspoon salt

Cilantro Sauce

1 cup cilantro, thick stems removed

½ cup plain yogurt

¼ cup red wine vinegar

¼ cup extra virgin olive oil

2 teaspoons Dijon mustard

2 cloves garlic

½ teaspoon each smoked paprika, cumin, black pepper

Potatoes: Preheat oven to 425°F. Cut potatoes in half lengthwise, then place cut side down on a parchment-lined baking sheet. Prick each potato in a few places with a fork. Bake for 30 to 45 minutes, or until fork tender. Remove potatoes but leave oven on when finished.

Filling: Heat oil in a large saute pan over medium heat. Add onion, pepper, and garlic, cooking until onion is soft and translucent, about 5 minutes. When finished, stir in corn and beans.

Scoop: Once sweet potatoes are cooked, pick up each half (using a paper towel to keep your hand from burning) and scoop out the flesh, leaving about ¼ inch on all sides to act as the bowl for your fillings. Transfer scooped out sweet potato flesh to a medium bowl, and combine it with the sour cream, minced adobo peppers, and salt.

Assemble: Fold together the veggie mixture with the sour cream mixture. Stuff each hollowed potato with filling. (You will have leftover filling.*)

Bake: Place stuffed sweet potatoes back onto the baking sheet and bake for 10 minutes.

Sauce: Blend all Cilantro Sauce ingredients until smooth (if you have a handheld immersion blender or small blender use it here–sometimes the small ingredient amounts make this recipe tricky for larger blenders).

Serve warm, topped with cilantro sauce!

**See next page for what to do with leftover filling →*

VEGAN (use vegan sour cream and yogurt), **GLUTEN-FREE**

per serving: calories 565 | carbs 82.3g | fiber 15.1g | sugar 6.4g | protein 12g | fat 22.3g | sodium 561mg | iron 3mg

Enchilada Stuffed Sweet Potatoes ...continued

The leftover filling mixture from the Enchilada Stuffed Sweet Potatoes is excellent for making fritters! These can be served over a bed of greens, on a bun like a burger, or as a savory breakfast.

Stir 1 egg and about ¼ cup of flour (or enough to make dough shapable) into the leftover mixture.

Shape into patties or scoop it directly into the pan and flatten with a spatula.

Cook in an oiled pan until both sides are golden brown.

Have a question about this recipe?

"We made this last night for the first time. It's seriously delicious. Unprompted, my honey – a carnivore – rated it 5/5"

-Elle

Have a question about this recipe?

Chickpea Pot Pie

A pot pie can certainly be a labor of love (like in middle school when my mom—to outdo Marie Callender—would make individually portioned pot pies for me to bring as school lunch). This pot pie is all the love without the labor. Prep the filling in a cast iron on the stove, then top with crust and pop it right into the oven.

SERVES 6 • 1 HOUR

1 pie dough (for classic crust) or puff pastry (for flaky crust)

1 large egg

Veggie Filling

1 tablespoon olive oil

¼ cup diced white or yellow onion, about ¼ medium onion

2 cloves garlic, minced

1 cup chopped carrots, about 2 medium carrots

½ cup corn

½ cup chopped celery, about 1 stalk

1 cup fresh or frozen peas

2 (15-ounce) cans chickpeas, drained

Sauce

¼ cup unsalted butter

¼ cup + 2 tablespoons all-purpose flour

½ teaspoon salt

¼ teaspoon black pepper

2 cups vegetable broth

½ cup heavy cream

Pastry: Whether using pie dough or puff pastry, set it on the counter to bring to room temperature. Whisk egg and set aside.

Veggies: Preheat oven to 400°F. Heat oil in a large cast iron skillet over medium heat. Add onion, garlic, carrots, corn, and celery. Cook until veggies are tender and brightly colored, about 10 minutes. Transfer veggies to a bowl and wipe pan clean. Stir frozen peas and chickpeas into veggies.

Sauce: Melt butter in the cast iron skillet over medium heat. Whisk in the flour, salt, and pepper, cooking until flour loses its raw floury smell, about 2 minutes. Slowly whisk in broth, and cook for 3 to 4 minutes, until thickened. Remove from heat then whisk in cream. Stir veggies into the sauce.

Assemble: Top cast iron skillet with your pastry (either woven into strips or the entire dough covering the pie with slits cut in it to vent hot air). Trim the edges or tuck dough inside the pan. Brush with egg and transfer to oven (put a large baking sheet on a rack below to protect against leaks.)

Bake for 30 minutes, or until crust is golden brown. Let rest for 15 minutes before digging in.

No Cast Iron?

You can cook the fillings in a regular skillet, then transfer everything to a casserole or pie dish!

per serving: calories 447 | carbs 51.2g | fiber 8.3g | sugar 4g | protein 13.6g | fat 22g | sodium 1006mg | iron 3mg

"My family loved this recipe! They've asked for it to be in our regular rotation of meals."

-Becky

Have a question about this recipe?

Crispy Baked Tofu Nuggets

Nuggets! Not just for kids. Flavorful marinated tofu is torn into uneven chunks to resemble chicken nuggets, then dunked into a crispy breading and baked. For the tofu skeptics, this recipe is a great starting point.

SERVES 4 • 1 HOUR 30 MINUTES

1 (14-ounce) block firm or extra firm tofu

Marinade

2 tablespoons nutritional yeast

2 tablespoons soy sauce

2 tablespoons apple cider vinegar

2 tablespoons olive oil

Breading

½ cup all-purpose flour

2 tablespoons cornstarch

½ cup almond milk

1 teaspoon apple cider vinegar

1 cup panko breadcrumbs

1 tablespoon nutritional yeast

2 teaspoons each garlic powder, onion powder, smoked paprika

½ teaspoon each salt and pepper

To cook: oil or cooking spray

Press: Press tofu for at least 15 minutes, using either a tofu press or by setting a heavy pan on top of it and letting the moisture drain. When finished, dry then tear tofu into roughly bite-sized blocks.

Marinate: In a shallow dish, stir together all Marinade ingredients. Add tofu and toss to coat. Let tofu marinate for at least 30 minutes (up to 24 hours).

Breading Station: Preheat oven to 400°F. In a medium bowl stir together flour and cornstarch. In a second bowl whisk almond milk and apple cider vinegar to make a "buttermilk". Combine breadcrumbs and all remaining seasonings in a third bowl.

Bread: Working one at a time, use a fork to dip each tofu nugget first in the flour, then almond milk, then breadcrumbs. Place on a parchment-lined baking sheet. Spray or brush each lightly with cooking oil to help them brown in the oven.

Bake for 25 minutes, flipping each over after 10 minutes of cooking.

Air fry it

To air fry tofu nuggets, place them in a single layer in your air fryer. Cook at 400°F for 10 to 15 minutes, or until golden brown and crispy.

VEGAN

per serving: calories 402 | carbs 42.2g | fiber 4.4g | sugar 3.4g | protein 23g | fat 16.8g | sodium 969mg | iron 1mg

Have a question about this recipe?

Roasted Cabbage Steaks With Lemon Tahini Sauce

Cabbage is a great gateway vegetable for people on the fence about the whole eating-vegetables-thing. Cabbage becomes buttery and tender when roasted, with crispy edges bringing a little charred flavor. Any bitterness in the cabbage is balanced by the lemony, garlic-infused tahini sauce.

SERVES 4 • 45 MINUTES

Steaks

2 heads green cabbage

¼ cup olive oil

½ teaspoon each salt, smoked paprika, garlic powder, onion powder

Sauce

¼ cup lemon juice

2 cloves garlic, minced

½ cup tahini

2 teaspoons Dijon mustard

½ teaspoon salt

¼ to ½ cup cold water

Prep: Preheat oven to 400°F. Peel any damaged outer leaves off of the cabbage, leaving the stems intact. Cut each head vertically into 4 or 5 slabs, about 1 inch thick. Stir together olive oil and seasonings, then brush onto both sides of each cabbage steak.

Roast: Set each piece onto a parchment-lined baking sheet. Bake for about 30 minutes, flipping once halfway through cooking, or until cabbage steaks are tender and browned at the edges.

If you find that the cabbage is browning too quickly, cover the whole pan with aluminum foil to help tenderize it without burning.

Sauce: While the cabbage cooks, stir together lemon juice and garlic. Let sit for 10 minutes to allow garlic flavor to infuse into the lemon juice. Use a mesh sieve to strain out garlic pulp, keeping the lemon juice. Whisk together the garlicky lemon juice, tahini, mustard, salt, and water (adding more until it reaches a smooth consistency).

Serve: Drizzle sauce over hot cabbage steaks before serving.

VEGAN, GLUTEN-FREE

per serving: calories 269 | carbs 28g | fiber 12g | sugar 14.6g | protein 7.2g | fat 2.6g | sodium 462mg | iron 3mg

Have a question
about this recipe?

Buddha's Delight (Lo Han Jai)

Buddha's Delight is a Chinese recipe served during the Chinese New Year. Its ingredients vary but often include dried shiitake mushrooms, dried lily buds, and bean curds (to name a few). This recipe is not an authentic version, but instead one that can be cooked using ingredients found in most Western pantries.

SERVES 4 • 35 MINUTES

Veggies

1 tablespoon olive oil

6 cups chopped veggies (can include mushrooms, bok choy, broccoli, snow peas, carrots, bell peppers)

¼ teaspoon each salt and pepper

Sauce

1 tablespoon toasted sesame oil

1 tablespoon grated ginger

3 cloves garlic, minced

¼ cup soy sauce

1 tablespoon honey

Assembly

1 tablespoon olive oil

8 ounces seitan, cut into bite-sized pieces

1 (8-ounce) can bamboo shoots, drained

To serve: sliced green onions, sesame seeds

Veggies: Heat oil in a large saute pan or wok (the largest you have) over medium/high. Add veggies, salt, and pepper. Cook until veggies are slightly softened and browning at the edges, 8 to 10 minutes.

Sauce: Meanwhile, add sesame oil to a small pan over medium heat. Add ginger and garlic, cooking until soft and fragrant, about 2 minutes. Stir in soy sauce and honey to warm, then remove from heat.

Seitan: Remove veggies from the large saute pan and add another 1 tablespoon of oil. Heat over medium/high, then add seitan. Cook, shaking often, until seitan is golden brown, 5 to 7 minutes.

Assemble: To the pan with the seitan add back in the veggies, bamboo shoots, and sauce. Toss to evenly combine. Serve warm, topped with sliced green onions and sesame seeds.

What is seitan?

Also known as "wheat meat," seitan is a popular meat substitute made from gluten, the protein found in wheat. It has a chewy texture that can mimic the taste and texture of meat.

VEGAN (replace honey with brown sugar)

per serving: calories 244 | carbs 20.3g | fiber 4.8g | sugar 10g | protein 18.6g | fat 11.5g | sodium 1391mg | iron 3mg

"I'm not usually a fan of quinoa but I took a chance on this recipe because I like being open minded. I'm so glad I did! Loved this full of flavor salad. A new favorite for sure."

-Elizabeth

Have a question about this recipe?

Lemony Arugula Grain Bowls

By using lemon zest (for flavor) and lemon juice (for acidity), these bowls taste like pure sunshine. Thanks to the quinoa—a complete source of proteins—and navy beans, each serving packs in 17 grams of protein and 12 grams of fiber, meaning these will keep you satisfied for a while!

SERVES 4 • 30 MINUTES

- 1 cup uncooked quinoa
- 1 lemon
- 2 tablespoons extra virgin olive oil
- 2 cloves garlic, minced
- 1 teaspoon Dijon mustard
- Pinch of salt and pepper
- 4 handfuls arugula
- ½ cup cubed feta cheese
- 1 (15-ounce) can navy beans, drained and rinsed
- ¼ cup pistachios, shelled and roughly chopped

Quinoa: Cook quinoa according to instructions on the package.

Lemon: Meanwhile, grate the zest off of half of the lemon and reserve. Juice the lemon and divide juice in half.

Arugula: In a large bowl, whisk together half of the lemon juice, oil, garlic, mustard, and a pinch of salt and pepper. Toss in the arugula.

Season Quinoa: When quinoa is finished cooking, fluff it with a fork then fold in the lemon zest, remaining lemon juice, and a pinch of salt and pepper.

Assemble: Into 4 serving bowls, layer the quinoa, arugula, feta, beans, and pistachios.

VEGAN (omit feta), **GLUTEN-FREE**

per serving: calories 414 | carbs 50g | fiber 11.6g | sugar 2g | protein 16.6g | fat 17.7g | sodium 439mg | iron 4mg

"Delicious, silky, spicy flavors. Amazing! So yummy I am licking up the pan with naan!"

-Kari

Have a question about this recipe?

Vegan Butter Chicken

A flavorful Indian-inspired classic turned vegan! With chewy baked tofu and a rich, velvety sauce, this is our go-to when craving takeout. The seasoned tofu is torn into chunks to resemble chicken. While that bakes, whip together the sauce on the stove. Bonus: It tastes even better the next day (hello, meal prep!)

SERVES 4 • 1 HOUR

Tofu

2 (14-ounce) blocks firm or extra firm tofu

2 tablespoons cornstarch

1 teaspoon each salt, curry powder

Sauce

2 tablespoons coconut oil

1 cup diced yellow onion, about 1 medium onion

1 tablespoon grated ginger

4 cloves garlic, minced

1 tablespoon each garam masala, ground coriander

1 teaspoon Kashmiri chili powder*

½ teaspoon each salt, cumin

1 (13-ounce) can full-fat coconut milk

1 (6-ounce) can tomato paste

To serve: basmati rice, naan

* or use ¾ teaspoon sweet paprika and ¼ teaspoon cayenne

Rice: If serving with rice, start cooking rice now and cover to keep warm when finished.

Prep Tofu: Preheat oven to 425°F. Drain the tofu then wrap it in clean towels and set something heavy on it for 20 or so minutes (if you have a tofu press, use that). Pat dry and tear into bite-sized chunks. In a large bowl, combine cornstarch, curry powder, and salt. Toss in the tofu, gently stirring to evenly coat.

Bake: Arrange tofu on a greased baking sheet and cook for 25 to 30 minutes, flipping each piece halfway through cooking.

Flavor Base: Meanwhile, heat coconut oil in a large saute pan or pot over medium heat. Add onion and cook, stirring often, until onion is very soft and translucent, about 10 minutes. Stir in ginger and garlic, and continue cooking for 1 minute. Stir in garam masala, coriander, kashmiri chili powder, salt, and cumin.

Sauce It: Stir in coconut milk and tomato paste. Cover and gently simmer for 15 minutes to reduce the acidity from the tomato paste, stirring occasionally. It will be dark orange when done. Optionally blend your sauce (either with a handheld immersion blender or by carefully transferring to a counter top blender—never tightly close when blending hot liquids; leave lid cracked to allow steam to escape!)

Serve: Stir tofu into the sauce and serve warm with naan and rice.

VEGAN, GLUTEN-FREE

per serving: calories 333 | carbs 22g | fiber 5g | sugar 6.7g | protein 23g | fat 19.7g | sodium 1000mg | iron 5mg

Tabbouleh Salad, page 58
(served with hummus and pita)

6

Meal Prep Ideas

Planning and prepping meals in advance is an incredibly efficient and budget-friendly way of eating (plus, it ensures you get a delicious, homemade meal on the table rather than grabbing fast food or takeout).

The concept is simple: make a few meals ahead so you can grab a premade meal and enjoy it when you need to eat. While we love it for vegetarian lunches, meal prep is also easy for vegetarian dinners.

meal prep ideas

Stuffed Avocados

SERVES 1 to 2 • 15 MINUTES

1 avocado

Filling Ideas

Israeli Sunshine Salad, page 53
Summer Veggie Salad, page 54
Mexican Bean Salad, page 59
Chickpea "Tuna", page 75
Lemony Arugula Grain Bowls, page 147

Filling: Choose the filling of your choice and prepare it. (Each will make enough to stuff about five avocados. I recommend ½ to 1 avocado per serving.)

Cut Avocado: When ready to eat, cut avocado in half lengthwise, making sure to not cut through the seed. Twist each half in opposite directions to create 2 halves. Place the half with the seed on a firm surface. Carefully thwack your knife into the seed, twisting the knife to pop the seed out.

Stuff: Stuff your filling into the well of each avocado half, enjoying it straight from the avocado with a fork or spoon!

VEGAN (options), **GLUTEN-FREE**

THAI COCONUT CURRY WITH TOFU

PAGE 49

ROASTED BUTTERNUT CHICKPEA WRAPS

PAGE 85

ROASTED CHICKPEA GYROS

PAGE 73

TIKKA MASALA INSPIRED CHICKPEAS

PAGE 131

Meal Prep Combos

I've included some of my favorite meal prep combinations here, using recipes from the book that hold up well when cooked in advance or when the meal's components are prepared in advance to make assembly a breeze at meal time. These are great for making several single-serve lunches or a dinner in advance for the crew!

PAGE 103 Stuffed Peppers

+

PAGE 53 Israeli Salad

PAGE 113 Lasagna

+

PAGE 54 Summer Veggie Salad

PAGE 91 Bean & Cheese Tacos

+

PAGE 55 Mexican Street Corn

PAGE 141 Tofu Nuggets

+

PAGE 56 Chickpea Corn Salad

PAGE 79 Bánh Mì

PAGE 57 Thai Cucumber Salad

PAGE 73 Chickpea Gyros

PAGE 58 Tabbouleh

PAGE 97 Sweet Potato Tacos

PAGE 59 Bean Salad

PAGE 133 Lemon Pepper Tofu

PAGE 67 Mediterranean Veggies

PAGE 75 Chickpea Tuna Melt

PAGE 52 Zucchini Corn Salad

Ingredient Index

Looking to cook with a specific ingredient? Use this ingredient index to find a recipe that features it! We've included primary ingredients here, leaving out aromatics used in most recipes (like onion or garlic) and ingredients like soy sauce or vinegar.

Thank You's

This book would have been impossible without my biggest supporters—my parents. They helped format and edit every page of this book, turning this crazy idea of a self-published cookbook into a reality (on a timeline that would have scared anyone else away). Moreover, this book would have been impossible had they not supported my crazy idea of running a food blog instead of a stable career path from the beginning. I am so lucky to have them.

And to Patrick, for being my unwavering support when all I worked on or talked about from morning until night was this cookbook. And thank you for letting me feed you so, so many chickpeas.

There's a small team of contractors behind Live Eat Learn who help me get recipes out to you every week. Thank you, Mika, Mitch, and Justine, for everything you do to help grow our little corner of the internet. Huge thanks also to the team at Foodie Digital, who maintain my site, my content strategy, and my sanity. Live Eat Learn wouldn't be where it is without you.

But this book truly wouldn't be here without YOU! Thank you for cooking my recipes, for sending me photos of your creations, for leaving reviews and comments, and for picking up this book. I'm so happy you're here.

Happy cooking,
Sarah

Sarah Bond is the vegetarian food blogger behind the popular website, Live Eat Learn. She uses her degrees in nutrition and food science to inspire healthy, approachable recipes (that don't compromise on flavor). A traveler at heart based in Denver, her experiences around the globe give rise to unique and delicious flavor combinations.

live eat learn

@liveeatlearn | www.LiveEatLearn.com

Visit my other sites:

www.BoneAppetreat.com
Dog Treat Recipes

www.BrewBuch.com
Kombucha Brewing Made Easy